E635
8367

-0. AUG 1978

338.646 | 5103499 | J.942.4
BENNETT

Please renew/return this item by the last date shown.

So that your telephone call is charged at local rate, please call the numbers as set out below:

L.32.

	From Area codes 01923 or 0208:	From the rest of Herts:
Renewals:	01923 471373	01438 737373
Enquiries:	01923 471333	01438 737333
Minicom:	01923 471599	01438 737599

L32b

4863 TELEX 81512

THE WORSHIPFUL COMPANY OF WHEELWRIGHTS OF THE CITY OF LONDON
1670–1970

TOAST OF THE COMPANY

*The Worshipful Company of
Wheelwrights—Root and Branch
—May it continue and flourish
for ever*

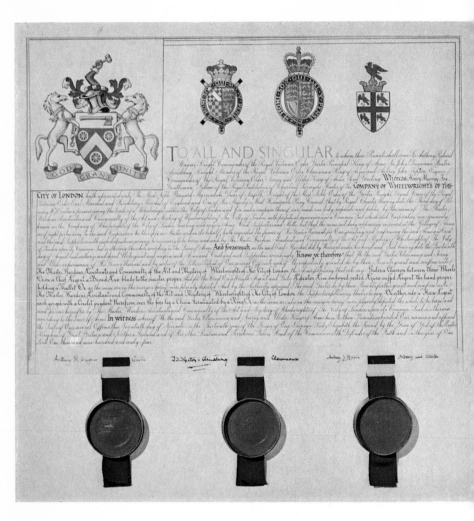

The Charter of the Company

ERIC BENNETT

The Worshipful Company
of Wheelwrights
of the City of London
1670-1970

DAVID & CHARLES : NEWTON ABBOT

ISBN 0 7153 4936 8

Set in eleven on thirteen point Baskerville
and printed in Great Britain
by Latimer Trend & Company Limited
for David & Charles (Publishers) Limited
South Devon House Newton Abbot Devon

Contents

Illustrations

Preface

THIS HISTORY has been written at the request of the Tercentenary Committee of the Worshipful Company of Wheelwrights of London. I should like to express my thanks to the Committee and to Mr Michael Hinton, FCA, Clerk to the Company, for his enthusiasm and assistance; to Past Master Leonard Norris, LLB, for providing some records hitherto thought irretrievably lost; and to Mrs Joan St George Saunders for her invaluable assistance in research.

ERIC BENNETT

Tercentenary Committee of the Worshipful Company of Wheelwrights

Dr Geoffrey Sturt Udall, MA, MB, B Chir, DCH, Chairman
Alderman H. Murray Fox, MA, FRICS, FAI
Richard Edwin Stubington, FCA
Hubert Sydney Dodson
Frank Geoffrey Wills, TD
Ex officio: F. Griffiths Woollard, DL, JP (Master 1968)
Duncan Thomas Russell (Renter Warden 1970)
Co-opted: William F. Newbury, FCIS, FCWA
Michael H. Hinton, FCA, CC (Clerk)

I

The Wheelwrights' Craft

ALTHOUGH THE Worshipful Company of Wheelwrights of the City of London has been in existence for only 300 years, yet the 'art and mistery' of the wheelwright's craft are amongst the oldest known to man. The method of making wheels for horse-drawn vehicles was unchanged in its essentials for 4,000 years, but with the development of first the bicycle and then the motor car, not only did the craft become almost extinct, but also its very language has been forgotten. Since the Wheelwrights Company was constantly concerned with enforcing and complying with laws about the manufacture of wheels, a large part of its history would be incomprehensible to a modern reader without an explanation of the methods used and of the technical terms of the trade. George Sturt added a glossary to his classic book *The Wheelwright's Shop*, and if that was necessary in 1923, I make no apology for prefacing this history with a short account of the wheel and the ways of the wheelwright.

The origins of the wheel are lost in the mists of prehistoric times. It is probable that even in the Stone Age men realised that a rolling stone or a round log of wood moved more easily than an object which had to be pulled or pushed. The first wheels were simply solid discs, carved out of one lump of wood.

Solid wheels made from three shaped planks followed, and the earliest examples of these date from about 5000 BC. They were discovered in Mesopotamia, but wheels of this type spread rapidly through Asia Minor and into Europe.

Solid wheels had two disadvantages: they were heavy and they broke across the grain of the wood. The problem was how to lighten the wheel and yet retain its strength. The answer came with the spoked wheel, which was certainly in existence in

Asia Minor by 2000 BC. The rims of the early spoked wheels were made of one piece of wood, bent in a full circle by a steaming process. The rim was connected to the hub, known to wheelwrights as the nave or stock, by wooden spokes. An Egyptian chariot wheel from Thebes, dating from 1435 BC, has a rim consisting of one piece of ash, curled full circle, and the spokes are morticed into the rim and the nave.

Steaming the wood to make it supple enough to bend in a circle must also have caused weakness, and the next invention was the felloe or felly. This was a curved wooden segment of a wheel rim. The felloes were joined together by dowels, and each felloe was morticed to take two spokes. With the knowledge of metal working, first in the Bronze Age and later in the Iron Age, wheels were further strengthened by tyres and nave bonds (small bands of iron clamped round the hub, one in front of the spokes and one behind).

Tyres were not then complete hoops. They were pieces of iron, curved by heat, and nailed across the joints of the felloes. The iron pieces were called strakes or shoes. From the earliest times in England wheels with iron strakes were referred to as being shod. Tyres made of a single piece of iron, heated and curved to form a hoop, did not exist in Britain before the last quarter of the eighteenth century and carts with straked wheels still existed in 1890.

Homer, writing about 1000 BC or even earlier, referred to wheels in terms the wheelwrights, who formed their Company in the seventeenth century, would readily have understood. Here, in Chapman's translation of the *Iliad*, is his description of the goddess Hera's chariot:

> Her golden-bridled steeds
> Then Saturn's daughter brought abroad; and Hebe, she proceeds
> T' address her chariot; instantly she gives it either wheel,
> Beamed with eight spokes of sounding brass; the axle-tree was steel;
> The fellies incorruptible gold, their upper bands of brass,
> Their matter most unvalued, their work of wondrous grace;
> The naves, in which the spokes were driven, were all with silver bound.

Except that they were working with more commonplace materials, the seventeenth-century wheelwrights, and their successors, were making their wheels in exactly the same way. But there was one important improvement. About a hundred years before the wheelwrights of London made their first petition for incorporation, the dished wheel had appeared. Dished wheels were shaped like saucers, with the hollow side outwards. The spokes were driven into the nave at an angle, so that when the lowest spoke stood perpendicularly to the load, the upper part of the wheel was sloping away from the body of the cart or carriage. This produced two advantages. It enabled the body of the vehicle to be wider at the top than at the floor, and it helped the wheel to withstand the lateral thrust of the axle caused by the action of the horse. To quote George Sturt:

> The loaded body of cart or waggon, swinging to the horse's stride, becomes a sort of battering-ram into the wheels, first this side and then that. It slides to and fro, on well-greased arms, right into the nave of each wheel. Now the off-side wheel gets a ramming, and promptly throws the weight back to the nearside. And so it goes on with every horse, all day long. The wheels have to stand not only the downward weight of the load; a perpetual thrust against them at the centre is no less inevitable.

He adds:

> I saw wheels turned inside out—like an umbrella in a wind— where the dish was too feeble.

But too much dishing was equally weakening to the wheel, and it was one of the earliest concerns of the Wheelwrights Company to inspect the wheels made by its members and to fine those who had made wheels 'too dishing'.

Wheelwrights were clearly craftsmen of a high order. They apparently used no mathematical formulas nor even drawings, but passed on the acquired knowledge of their craft from father to son, from master to apprentice. But patterns were used for felloes; for the bottom timbers of a wagon; for a dung cart; and a raved cart. (Raves were side rails added to a cart or wagon to allow a bigger load to be carried over the wheels.)

There were also traditional patterns for wagon shafts, cart shafts, tail-board rails; indeed, for every part of a cart, wagon, timber carriage and other vehicles—for all these were part of the wheelwright's trade.

The quality of the wheelwright's skill and the variety of his craft were not, of course, always appreciated. Campbell in *The London Tradesman* (1747) is disparagingly snobbish:

> The Coachmaker is a genteel, profitable Business both to Master and Journeyman; but requires a great Stock of Ready Money to set up and continue Trade; they deal with none but Nobility and Quality and according to their Mode must trust a long time, and sometimes may happen never to be paid.
>
> The Wheelwright is employed in making wheels for all manner of Carriages; I mean the wooden work. This business requires more Labour than Ingenuity; a Boy of a weakly Constitution can make no hand at this Trade. It is abundantly profitable to the Master and a Journeyman earns from 15 to 20s. a week. A Youth may be bound about Fifteen.
>
> The Cart-Wheeler differs nothing from the Coach Wheeler, but that he makes wheels for carts only and is not obliged to turn his work so neatly finished as the other.
>
> A Boy designed for this trade requires to be of strong robust Constitution and ought not to be bound till the age of 15 or 16, when his joints begin to knit and he has arrived at a moderate degree of strength. A Journeyman earns from 12 to 15s. a week.

Campbell also mentions tyre-smiths as a separate trade, with journeymen earning 22s a week and an ordinary workman 15s. He puts the cost of an apprenticeship to a wheelwright as from £5 to £10 and the working hours from 6 am to 8 pm. The cost of setting up as a master wheelwright is reckoned at between £100 and £200.

More understanding reference to the wheelwright was made by *The Book of English Trades and Library of the Useful Arts* (1818):

> This artizan's employment embraces the making of all sorts of wheels for carriages which are employed in husbandry, as well as those adapted to the purposes of pleasure. Road waggons and other vehicles constructed for burden are also the manufacture of the wheelwright.
>
> In London this business is divided into two distinct branches of work; one of which being confined to the purpose of manufacturing

The Wheelwrights' Craft:
(*above*) Boring the spoke
holes in the nave or hub;
(*right*) driving in the spokes

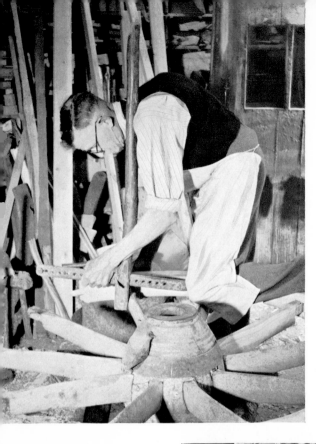

The Wheelwrights' Craft:
(*above*) Fitting the felloes,
using a spoke-dog; (*right*)
the fitted felloes begin to
form the rim

wheels for carriages of pleasure, is an appendage to coach-making;
the other to the making of the bodies, wheels, &c. of the different
kinds of machines required for the transport of the various com-
modities for the purposes of trade, and the comfort and convenience
of the people.

It will appear, by a very superficial examination, that such a
business is of very great consideration, and must be undoubtedly
of very great antiquity. . . .

It is pleasing to reflect, that, amidst all the various improve-
ments in arts and manufactures, this of carriage wheels has by no
means been neglected; our artizans in this line stand pre-eminent;
our carriages are manufactured on better principles, as well as
more neat in the execution, than are to be found in any other
country.

The eleventh edition of this book, published in 1823, has an
illustration of a wheelwright shoeing a wheel with a red-hot
strake; yet the text says:

The wheelwright's axe has a bended blade, and is used for
hollowing out the fellies. [The writer is really referring to an adze.]
By thus scooping out the wood, the grain is often so much cut and
injured as to weaken it in a great degree. To remedy this a method
has been invented of bending timber into a circular form, so that
the whole rim of the wheel consists of not more than two pieces,
which are covered with a tyre in a single piece. By this mode of
construction, the circumference of the wheel is every where
equally strong, and much more durable than wheels made in the
usual form.

So the wheel really had turned full circle—going back to a
method at least 4,000 years old. But, in fact, wheels with five,
six or seven felloes were still being made in this century.

The wheel began with the nave, usually a well-seasoned
piece of elm, lyrically described by Sturt:

A lumpish cylinder in shape—eleven or twelve inches in dia-
meter and twelve or thirteen inches from end to end—a newly-
turned stock was a lovely thing. . . . And now it lay, butter-
coloured, smooth, slightly fragrant, soon to begin years of field
work, after much more skill—the skill of ancient England—had
been bestowed on it, though already telling of that skill in every
curve.

Naves were originally rough-hewn with an axe, but were
later turned on a lathe. The wheelwright marked out the
places where the spokes were to be morticed into the nave, and

B

bored the holes for them. The spokes were of oak, and had been shaped by axe, saw and spoke-shave to have the maximum of strength with the minimum of weight. They were driven into the nave with a sledge hammer, not straight, but at an angle to give the right amount of dish.

The felloes, of ash, elm, oak or beech, had been shaped to pattern and were then bored to take the tongues of the spokes: two spokes to each felloe. They were also bored to take the dowel of the adjacent felloe. Once they were hammered into position the wheel had its rim.

For shoeing, the wheel was set up over a pit of water. The wheelwright took out the strip of iron, already curved by heat and punched with nail-holes, and laid it red hot on the top of wheel rim. As the hot iron burned into the wood, the wheelwright punched in his big rose-headed nails, and then turned the wheel round into the pit of water. While the newly-fastened strake was cooling, the operation was repeated on the opposite side of the wheel, until the six strakes completed the job of tyring.

Hoop tyres, solid bars of iron bent into a full circle and welded, were put on hot and nailed into position on the wheel rim. As the tyre cooled and shrank, it pulled the spokes into exactly the right amount of dish. The nave bonds were then put on hot and driven into place.

Finally, the wheel had to be boxed. This meant that the centre of the nave had to be hollowed out and a cast-iron box inserted and fixed with wedges. Into this box the axle-arm was fitted. Under the first Bylaws of the Worshipful Company it was a punishable offence to sell wheels before they had been boxed and shod.

For most wheelwrights, however, wheels were only part of their work. They often built the cart or wagon, complete with shafts and axle-beds; it would then be their responsibility to see that the wheels were properly hung on the axle-arms. The iron axle-arms were given a slight downward and forward slope, so that in a dished wheel the lowest spoke, which was at that moment taking the full weight of the load, stood perpendicular.

So much for the craft and the age-old tradition of the wheel-wright. Homer's chariot wheel had eight spokes, but Chaucer in *The Somnours Tale* (*c.* 1388) wrote:

> Lat bringe a cartwheel here into this halle,
> but loke that it have his spokes alle.
> Twelf spokes hath a cartwheel comunly.

It continued to have twelve spokes, until it was replaced by the tractor and trailer or the motor van. A cart, it must be noted, was always a two-wheeled vehicle. A wagon had four wheels and, for the convenience of turning, the front wheels were smaller than the hind wheels.

Shakespeare, who died fourteen years before the Wheel-wrights of London made their first petition for incorporation, mentions wheels in *Hamlet*—from which are taken the last words of this chapter, spoken by First Player:

> Out, out, thou strumpet Fortune! All you gods,
> In general synod, take away her power;
> Break all the spokes and fellies from her wheel,
> And bowl the round nave down the hill of heaven,
> As low as to the fiends!

2

One Body Corporate and Politique

EARLY IN the reign of Charles I, the Wheelwrights of London, having become wealthy enough to pay the costs and legal fees involved in incorporation, formed a committee to approach the City authorities. The first mention of them in the 'Repertories of the Court of Aldermen' is dated 20 January 1630:

> Item this day upon the humble petition of the Wheelwrights in and about the City of London It is ordered by this Court that Sir Heneage Finch Knight and Recorder Mr Alderman Parkhurst Mr Alderman Ffen Mr Alderman Wright Mr Common Sergeant Mr Stone Mr Greene and Mr Pheasant or any four of them whereof Mr Recorder to be one shall hear and consider of the petitions grievances and of their desire to be incorporated And certify unto this Court in writing under their hands how they find the same together with their doings and opinions And William Gunthroppe to warn and attend them.

In the following September the Court ordered that 'any four of the aforesaid committee shall pursue the said order' and on 6 March 1631, they reported:

> Item this day Alderman Parkhurst and Alderman Ffen and Alderman Wright & Mr Stone committees formerly appointed to consider of the petition and grievances of the Wheelwrights and Coachmakers did deliver unto this Court a report in writing under their hands how they find the same and to their doings and opinions in tenor whereof as follows viz
> To the right honble Lord Mayor of City of London
> and the right worshipful Aldermen of the same
> According to two several orders of this honourable Court . . . we have considered of the Wheelwrights and Coachmakers inhabiting the City of London & suburbs of the same and other adjacent places within the compass of seven miles and do find that many

frauds and deceits are daily used by the Wheelwrights and Coachmakers which do use in their works much young & unseasoned
timber which when it is fitted for wheels or frames for coaches are
shrunk and thereby being disjointed both coach and wheels
quickly decay whereby mens occasions in their journeys are
disappointed & their lives many times endangered

We find also that much deal wood in joint work of coaches is used
which breaketh with the shaking of the coach and that these abuses
by reason that the said coaches and wheels are painted and
coloured cannot easily be discovered but by men of those faculty
nor be reformed but by some politic constitutions prohibiting the
same And we find also that many green wheels are vended by
Bargmen and others which do often break in the streets of the
City and places adjacent to the damage and hurt of passengers And
whereas the Petitioners do desire from this Court a favourable
report whereby they may with more facility procure from his
Royal Majesty Letters patent to incorporate them the said Wheelwrights and Coachmakers into one body politic that so they may be
enabled to reduce the abuses aforesaid and suppress the exercise of
those trades in such as have not served as Apprentices thereunto
and so make bad and insufficient workmanship We conceiving
that Joiners & Smiths and others may be concerned therein and
therefore being willing to hear what they can say to the contrary
did cause many of the chief men of those misteries to appear before
us and to that many of them appearing none of them did oppose
the same but they all think that the abuses aforesaid may be the
better reformed by making the petitioners a corporation of which
opinion we are that they being incorporated they may have
power given them to make reasonable ordinances not repugnant
to the laws of this kingdom or liberty of this City provided that
the Blacksmiths be not restrained to sett on strakes and other iron
works upon the wheels as formerly they have done which the
Wheelwrights are very willing they should do All which we leave
to your honor and worships grave consideration

Robt Parkhurst
Robt Ffen
Edmund Wright
Jo Stone

The which Report being here openly read was allowed of and
ordered to be entered into the Repertory and to be accordingly
performed providing that they shall not molest or compel any
person or persons whatsoever free of any Company within this
City using the trade of a Wheelwright or Coachmaker to be
translated into their corporation and that such orders and ordinances as they shall hereafter make for the rule and good government of the said incorporation be allowed and approved of by
this Court.

So, it seemed set fair. Later that year (1630), the leading wheelwrights and coachmakers had come together and had petitioned for incorporation as a single company, but the City fathers were never in a hurry. On 10 January 1632 another committee was appointed by the Court of Aldermen:

> Item this day upon a motion made unto this Court by Mr Stone for and in the behalf of Wheelwrights and Coachmakers of this City and other adjacent places who have petition to be incorporated. It is thought fit and so ordered by this Court that the Recorder & Alderman Parkhurst & Alderman Ffen and Alderman Wright or any three of them shall hear and consider of the said petition and advise whether it may be fit to have the said petitioners incorporated as they desire or what is fit to be done for their relief And to certify unto to this Court in writing under their hands how they shall find the same and their doings and opinions And John Monger to warn and attend them.

That was the last heard of the joint petition of the wheelwrights and coachmakers. In the following thirty years or so, two civil wars, a war with the Dutch, the Great Plague and the Fire of London, were of more consequence to the citizens of London than the welfare of the wheelwrights. But at last their petition, made independently of the coachmakers, was heard with favour and on 3 February 1670 Charles II granted them a Charter. Its full text is given in Appendix I, page 130.

The first act of the new Company was to petition the Court of Aldermen 'to have their Charter enrolled and their Corporation to be owned as a member of this City'. This was duly allowed with the 'cautions and limitations' following:

> That they shall have no livery of their Company for choice of Mayor & Sheriffs or members of Parliam^t unless this honble Court shall hereafter by their positive order in writing grante and allow the same.
> That no member of any of the Company of this Citty following the Wheelrights trade shall be exempt from bearing office or paying duties to the Company of which they are now free shall notwithstanding this new Charter be continued to their Companies as formerly.
> That the said Company of Wheelwrights shall from time to time hereafter as they have occasion keep their Courts & meetings

within this City and Liberties & not in the suburbs or in any other place without the Liberties.

Since the first three Court Minute Books of the Company, covering the period from 1670 to 1766, were destroyed in World War II, it is impossible to give a detailed account of the formative years of the Wheelwrights. Fortunately, the extracts made from these books by the late James B. Scott (Clerk to the Company from 1870 to 1908) and published in his *Short Account of the Worshipful Company of Wheelwrights* in 1884, together with some scattered contemporary records enable us to follow the trend of the Company's early fortunes and the development of the trade.

The Company's first problem was raising the money to pay the charges for incorporation—a matter of £300. This was a considerable sum under any circumstances, but the absence of any fixed fines payable on admission, or of any fees payable by members joining the Court, made the raising of this amount very difficult. The only source of revenue at that time was the subscription—usually £5, and paid in instalments—paid by wheelwrights on joining the Company.

One of the earliest entries in the minute books is that of 27 May 1670: 'Mrs. Rand did this day promise to pay to this Company towards their charge of Incorporation on Midsomer day next the sum of 5£'. 'Mrs. Robinson did this day promise to pay to this Company the remainder of her Subscription on Midsomer day next.'

Women were admitted to the Freedom of the Company from the beginning and this practice continued well into the nineteenth century. Some were widows of wheelwrights who carried on the trade of their late husbands, others were admitted as apprentices and some by patrimony.

Admissions to the Freedom in those early days were made by the Court and, as James Scott points out, there was a certain amount of bargaining in the transaction. Thus:

> June 24th, 1670. Mrs. Hawkins of Bridewell, widd., did this day promise to the Company that if she doth continue her Trade six months longer, that then she will give as much towards the charge of the Company as other widdows doe.
> This day Mr Robert Methley appeared and desired to be

admitted a member of this Company, and some objections being then offered that he had not served by the space of seaven yeares to the Trade of a Wheelwright, hee did then promise to produce to this Court sufficient evidence of his seaven yeares service to the sd Trade within one fortnight, and then also to pay to the use of the Company the sum of 5£.

And again:

July 8th, 1670. This day Mr Edward Bussey, appearing upon summons before the Court, and desiring to be admitted a member of this Company, it was put to the question by reason of some objections which were by some persons offered against his admittance, and thereupon carried in the affirmative by all the persons present except two, and thereupon hee was admitted, and promied to pay 5£ to the Company, wh. being thought too little, he promised 5£ more, and for anything more hee was left to his free-will.

Raising funds was not, however, the only difficulty. Francis Jesson, who had been appointed a Warden by the Royal Charter, refused to take up his office, and although repeatedly summoned, he did not appear. In 1672, he was summoned to appear before the Court of Aldermen 'to answer the matters alledged against him in the petition of the Masters Wardens and Assistants and loyalty of the Art or Mistery of Wheelwrights.' There is no record of his appearance. Under the by-laws of 1670, Francis Jesson was fined £10 by the Company and when he refused to pay the Court subscribed to pay for his prosecution. Again, there is no record of the result.

Henry Fotheringham, the first Beadle nominated in the Charter, was not elected to that office—although Scott does not say who took his place. Thomas Johnson, the first Clerk, was discharged in December 1672 for 'continually absenting himself'. The Court also ordered that his arrears of salary should not be paid until he had handed over all books, papers, writings and moneys belonging to the Company. When his successor was appointed, Johnson unsuccessfully claimed the office, but he did receive his arrears of salary. Five years later he was reinstated, 'so long as he executed the office in person', but in 1682 he was finally dismissed 'for severall reasons best knowne to ye Company'.

In spite of these troubles the Court began to organise the Company. In its first meetings at the 'Swan' in Old Change, at Cutler's Hall, and the 'Paul's Head', it was mainly concerned with admitting members and binding apprentices. Since the Charter allowed the Court to admit 'such person or persons as they shall from tyme to tyme think fitt and as shall desire to become members of the said Society', not all the new members were wheelwrights, and apprentices were often bound through the Company to learn other trades. The first apprentice was bound by the Company in September 1670.

Some of the Company's earliest regulations introduced fines for absence or late appearances at Court meetings and a fine of 6d imposed for 'coming to the Court with an apron before him or otherwise indecently habited'. This fine was paid to the Master for the use of the Beadle.

These regulations were confirmed, with some variations, by the first bylaws which were approved and signed on 12 October 1670 by the Lord Keeper of the Great Seal and the Chief Justices of the Courts of King's Bench and Common Pleas. The bylaws appointed the days for holding Courts of Assistants, made provision for quarterage on all members, laid down conditions of apprenticeship, of trading and workmanship, and decided the fees for admission. It also prescribed the penalties and fines for absenteeism and for refusal to take office. The bylaws are one of the foundation stones of the Company's control of its members and regulation of the trade. They are set out in full in Appendix II.

In 1671 the Company began to function fully. The first search or view, as provided for in the Charter, was made in April that year. In the first searches, one Warden or Assistant took the north side of the City and Liberties and the other the south side. Later there were more specific locations, such as the Whitechapel search, the Southwark search, and the St Giles's search. Warrants for these searches were generally obtained from the Recorder, and when members were found to be using inferior material or the work was not in accordance with the standards laid down, the goods were seized and fines imposed.

On one occasion, an action for trespass was brought against those engaged in a 'view' and the Clerk was ordered to appear in defence—but the outcome is not recorded.

The earliest extant record of a penalty for bad workmanship is dated 18 June 1674—incurred for selling wheels before they were shod or boxed. The penalty was 40s, with a threat of legal proceedings if not paid. Sometimes delinquents were dealt with at a special session of the Committee Court, such as that held on 24 February 1681—the Court comprising: Mr Emery, Master; Mr J. Jackson, Warden; Messrs Timberlake, Box, Duke and Eades. Seven members appeared before the Court: two were fined 7s 6d each; the rest 5s each. While six of these delinquents put themselves at the mercy of the Court, one word described the other—'refractory'.

Later that year a new regulation was made for the direction of the wheelwright's trade. On 8 December 1681 the Court ordered that:

> Every Cart from henceforth to be made for the said use, shall be in bodie of the same Cart between the staves thereof four feet of Assise and in length from the fore end of the shaft to the outside of the hinder Earebred thirteen foot four inches and noo more.
>
> And that the Wheeles of the said Carts be not made dishing beyond the face of the Wheele nave. And that the Sweepe of the said wheeles exceed not eight inches and nine inches in depth. And that noe Axeltree of any such Cart exceed three foote nine Inches in length under the bodies of the said Carts.

This regulation, together with the provisions against unsound workmanship in the 1670 bylaws, led to disciplinary actions by the Company:

> 17th May, 1688. This day Mr. Thomas Girdler appeareing in Court was accused for exposeing to sale sevrall coach wheeles made of unsound Timber, and that he being informed of the penalties that would fall upon him by vertue of the Bylawes of this Compaine, he the said Mr. Girdler did in a very unseemly manner revile this Compaine, and said that he cared not for the Bylawes. Upon hearing the whole complaint this Court did fine him in all four pounds for his rotten wheeles, but afterwards he declaring his sorrow for his offences and submitting himselfe to the Court his fine was remitted to 10s. wch he Payd, and his contempt was passed by.

At a Court of Committee Holden at Cutlers Hall, London, the 27th Aprill, 1692.

Memorand that the Master and other Members of this Compaine being since the last Court day upon the view, to search see whether the members of this Compaine did make theire Carrs Carts and Wheeles of Good Timber and workemanlike and according to the Rules and orders of this Compaine and upon theire search did find these persons following to have made theire Wheeles and Carts contrairie to the Rules and Orders (viz)

Mr. Hugh Emery for one wheel too Dishing
Mr. Thomas Jackson for makeing one wheele too Deepe
Mr. William Harman, for one wheele too Dishing.
Mr. James Kerby for one wheele too Dishing.
Mr. John Snellgrove, for one wheele too Dishing.
Mr. John Craddock &c. for one wheele too Dishing.
Mr. Thomas Gould for one wheele too Dishing.
Mr. Duck for one wheele too Dishing.

all wch said persons submitting themselves to the Board and it being putt to the vote what fines they should sevrally pay it was agreed that they should pay 2s. a peece it being theire first offence wch they paid

And Mr. Charles Hewitt being formerly an Offender in this kind for makeing a Cart an Inch and halfe too wide was fined 10s. wch he paid it being his second offence.

Eodem Die

Mr. Edward Richards was alsoe found to have made a paire of whelle two Inches too dishing, and he being sumoned to appeare at this Court to answere the same he stood in contempt therefore the Court doth order that he bee sumoned before the Lord Mayor to answere it.

Quis custodiet ipsos custodes? Four of these offenders were Past Masters of the Company: Hugh Emery, 1682; Thomas Jackson, 1683; Charles Hewitt, 1688; and William Harman, 1691. Another, James Kerby, was to serve as Master in 1698 and again in 1710.

The fining of Masters, Wardens and Assistants for breaking the rules about workmanship proves that the early 'searchers' were both fearless and vigilant. But the officers of the Company were sometimes in trouble for other reasons. In 1679 they were accused of forming a cartel to keep up prices and were summoned before the Court of Aldermen:

Thursday, 3rd March, 1679
James Trimblerley & others hereafter named having been Master Wardens or Assistants of the Company of Wheelwrights and being

> now convened before this Court upon Complaint made against
> them by several members of the said Company (which they like-
> wise have deposed) for a Combination to sitt & raise the prices of
> their work & taking bonds of the said persons upon their Admission
> into the said Company for paym^t of a sum of money but intended
> then as a means to oblige their observance of the said prices were
> therefore bound with sureties before Mr Recorder.

Those named in the combination with James Trimblerley
(or Timberly or Timberlake) were: Henry Graves, who became
Master in 1681; John King, Master in 1686; John Eades,
Master 1680; Hugh Emery, Master 1682; John Box, who had
been Master in 1677; Edward Wade, Master in 1690; Thomas
Morris, Henry Ray, Abraham Wright, Solomon Dealy,
William Pettifer and Henry Cooke. It is evident that the major
part of the Court of Assistants was involved.

Besides keeping the trade in order, the Court was much
exercised in collecting the Company's dues. The first quarterage was collected in 1671, when every Freeman had to pay 1s a
quarter and journeymen members 6d. Quarterage represented
the major part of the Company's income at this time, but
right from the beginning there was trouble in collecting it.
Indeed, as will be seen later, even Past Masters fell a long way
behind with their payments. As early as 1679 the Court had to
make an order:

> That the Master and Wardens for the time being shall issue
> out Warrts under the Comon Seale of this Society for seizeing the
> Goods of such persons Members of this Company who are or shall
> hereafter be refractory or refuse to pay their quarteridge or fines
> or other dues to this Company pursuant to the Charter and Bye-
> laws of this Corporation. And this Court and every Member
> thereof now present doe now promise to save harmlesse the person
> or persons that shall be imployed in executeing the same warrt.

The necessity for such action is evident from the early
minute books. For example, in January 1673: 'Mrs. Burgis, the
widdow of Mr. Richard Burgis, the late Warden of this Companie, did appear in Ct. and did positively refuse to pay her
proportion of the hundred pounds wch her husband wth others
was bound.' But in October, 1674, Mrs Burgis, whether under
pressure or not, had second thoughts:

This day Mr. Masters and Mr. Hardwick appeared in Court on the behalfe of Mrs. Burgis, and paid into Court the some of 5£ 10s. od. in full discharge of a bond her late husband entered into to Mr. Sherman, and thereupon this Ct did undertake to indempnifie her from any further damage or charges wch may happen to her by reason of the said bond.

Fines for non-attendance were also collected with some difficulty, and at one time the Company had to declare a partial amnesty:

> 31st October, 1678,
> It is this day unanimously agreed that whereas severall Members of this Court are guilty of many defaults in not attending the Service of this Company that for the time past they shall respectively pay the one Moiety of their defaults and the other Moiety to be buried in oblivion but for the future noe body to be Spared without lawfull Excuse.

At least one member put his dues in pawn to the Company:

> 25th September, 1679
> This day John Rugg pᵈ £1. 01. 06d. in full for Qtridge and other dues to the Company to Midsomer last inclusive and thereupon his Silver Tumbler was delivered to him.

The Company prosecuted not only members who had not paid their dues, but also wheelwrights who refused to join the Company or who had not served their apprenticeship to the trade. The cost of these proceedings was usually met by subscriptions from members of the Court.

Sometimes legal difficulties arose, and the Company was not always sure of its rights. In July 1674 the Wheelwrights petitioned the Court of Aldermen, 'desiring that all persons of their trade that shall hereafter come to take their freedom of this City may take the same only in the said Company and that all Apprentices to the said trade may be likewise bound only in the said Company'.

The petition was referred to a Committee, but there is no record of its findings. In the following year the Company itself resolved to bring journeymen into line:

> 15th July, 1675
> It is this day agreed upon and ordered by the consent of the whole Court That noe person who is or hereafter shall be a Mem-

ber of the Court of Assistants of this Compaine of Wheelewrights
or any other Freeman of the same Compaine or Fellowship shall
after the nine and twentieth day of September next (and haveing
notice of this Order) imploy any Journey: man wheelewright to
worke with him at the same Trade who shall refuse to be admitted
a freeman of this Corporation And that if any person being a
member of this Corporation shall imploy any Journeyman as
aforesd contrary to the Order aforesd, he shall forefeite and pay
to the use of this Company the summe of forty shillings for every
month that he shall imploy such Journeyman after he shall have
notice of this Order (unless leave be given by the Court of
Assistants of this Compaine), the same forfeitures to be paid in
like manner as other fines and forfeitures are appointed to be paid
by the Charter and By Lawes of this Compaine.

Meanwhile the Company had to deal with problems of
ethics, etiquette and finance:

27th June, 1672
It is Ordered by this Court That if any Wheeleright who is free
of this Compaine of Wheelwrights doe take another Wheelewrights Costomer from him (the same Customer being indebted
to that wheelewright that wrought to him) before such Customer
hath cleered his acc^{ts} wth that wheelewright that wrought to him
at the time when the Customer was taken from him, the ptie
soe doeing shall forfeit and pay the use of this Compaine the
Summe of five pounds in like manner as other fines and forfeitures
are appoynted to be paid by the By Lawes of this Compaine. And if
the ptie offending as aforesaid, be one of the Court of Assistants of
this Compaine, he shall not only forfeite and pay the Summe of
five pound as aforesaid but shall be discharged from the Office of
an Assistant of this Compaine.

As for etiquette:

21st October, 1675
Wheras a Complaint is made att this Board ag^{t} Robert Taverner
for abuseing all the Members of this Compaine wth his appro-
briouse Language, therefore the Court hath fined him 40s. And
the Beadle is ordered to summon him to appeare at the next Co^{t}
day to shew cause why he should not pay the same fine.
Ordered that every Assistant that shall smooke Tobacco in
Court roome During the sitting of the Court do each pay to the
use of the poor one shilling.

As for finance, money-raising was the Company's preoccupation throughout the formative years. The fine upon
admission to the Company allowed by the bylaws was only
13s 4d so the Company asked for further payments. Some paid

as much as £10, some refused to give any extra, and others promised to be 'further kind to the Company'.

One example of this is minuted under the date 9 February 1681: 'This Day John Norriss who served 7 yeares with Mr. William Craddock and his widdow, wass now made free & paid 13s. 04d. and promis^d to be as kind as others'.

Sometimes those petitioning for the freedom were only admitted if they paid an additional sum. Persons made free, but not immediately starting in trade, gave a bond for £5 in consideration of their doing so within the liberty of the Charter (see Appendix VII). This practice continued well into the eighteenth century.

As the number of voluntary gifts dwindled, the Court decided in 1680, to impose a fine for election on the Court of Assistants. The order stated that some members of the Court 'are at great charges for certain matters and others refuse to pay' and it fixed the fine at 50s. This was shortly afterwards raised to £10 and was confirmed in the supplementary by-laws.

The incorporation of the Wheelwrights naturally had some effect upon other Livery Companies and their members, raising controversy and sometimes individual hardship—when the judgment of the Court of Aldermen was invoked.

Tuesday, 29th November, 1687
    Upon a petition now presented to this Court by Wm Pettever Citizen and Currier desiring that, in regard he is by trade a Wheelwright and threatened to be molested by the Company of Wheelwrights unless he will become a Member of their Company, he may either be translated to the said Company or permitted to follow his trade without interruption. This Court doth intend to take that matter into consideration on this day sennight for the petitioners relief. And doth order that the Masters and Wardens of the said Companies do then make their appearance before the Court.

Tuesday, 6th December, 1687
    This day upon hearing a complaint made by Wm Pettever Citizen and Currier being also a Member of the Company of Wheelwrights that he is called upon to bear office and charge in both the said Companies Upon hearing of that matter (divers Members of both the said Companies being present) In regard the said Pettever was first admitted to the Company of Wheel-

wrights according to the said Companies Charter being by trade
a Wheelwright And that the burthen and charge of both the said
Companies will be too great a hardship upon him it is therefore
thought fit and ordered that he shall be translated from the Company of Curriers to the Company of Wheelwrights and that six
Members of either of the said Companies of Curriers Wheelwrights do appear before this Court for the translating of the said
Pettever accordingly.

Such translations were not infrequent in the first hundred
years of the Company's history. The Repertories of the Court
of Aldermen have the following entry for 12 January 1713:

> Upon the humble petition of John Linn and the report of Sir
> William Stewart and Sir George Marttin Knt and Alderman.
> That the Petitioner was bound as Apprentice to a Free Cloth-
> worker and hath a Right to his Freedom by Service in that Com-
> pany but being a Wheelwright by Trade is desirous to be made
> Free in the Company of Wheelwrights and the said Company of
> Clothworkers having had notice thereof and giving their consent
> thereunto It is ordered that the said John Linn shall be admitted
> into the Freedom of this City by Redemption in the said Company
> of Wheelwrights paying to Mr Chamberlain for the Citys use the
> sum of forty six shillings and eightpence.

Sometimes the request for translation was in reverse:

Shrove Tuesday, 18th February, 1738
> Upon reading the humble Petition of Robert Scowthroup setting
> forth that he was sometime since admitted into the Freedom of the
> City in the Company of Wheelwrights, and that he doth now and
> for some time past hath kept an Inn within this City, That by an
> Act of Common Council made the thirteenth of May 1663 (amongst
> other things) It is enacted that all and every person or persons of
> what company soever using the Art Mistery or Occupation of an
> Innholder or keeping or occupying any Inn Ostery or Livery
> Stable within this City or Liberties hereof should be from hence-
> forth translated from the Company wereof he was or should be
> free unto the said Company of Innholders and be sworn and
> admitted into the same. And praying to be translated accordingly.
> It is ordered that the Master and Wardens of the Company of
> Wheelwrights and the Master and Wardens of the Company of
> Innholders Do cause six of the Members of each Company respec-
> tively to attend this Court on Tuesday next in order to translate
> the said Robert Scowthroup from the said Company of Wheel-
> wrights to the said Company of Innholders according to the
> intent of the said Act.

The Wheelwrights' Craft: (*above*) Shaping the rim with an adze; (*right*) tyring a wheel

A wheelwright fixing the strakes to a wheel, from *The Book of English Trades and Library of the Useful Arts*, 1818

Similarly, in January 1743, Jonathan Frohock, Citizen and Wheelwright, was translated to the Innholders and six years later Francis Wilson, Citizen and Wheelwright, was translated to the Goldsmiths. It is interesting to note that Edward Bussey, to whose admission some members of the Court objected in the summer of 1670, became Master of the Company in 1684, and that John Linn, who chose to become a Wheelwright rather than a Clothworker in 1713, was elected Master in 1733.

Between 1670 and the end of the seventeenth century the Company made a number of regulations, which were confirmed with some variations by the supplementary bylaws of 1714 (see Appendix III).

In 1671 'for the better preservation of amity and brotherly love in the Society' it was ordered that four Stewards should be appointed every year to provide a dinner at their own expense, for the Court and their wives. But although the fine for refusing the office of Steward was £20, it was apparently difficult to find members who would undertake the task. In consequence, the Court decided in 1693 that there should be only two public dinners in a year: one at the Lady Day Quarter Court at the expense of the Company; the other at the Michaelmas Quarter Court, to be charged to the newly appointed Master and Wardens.

The following rules for the binding of apprentices, as applied to members of the Wheelwrights' Company, were made in 1683:

A member of the Company cannot keep more than one apprentice until that apprentice is in the last year of his apprenticeship, then he can take on another.

No wheelwright shall bind an apprentice until he has been five years out of his time and is in trade for himself.

Master Wardens and Assistants who are coach-wheelers shall not keep more than two apprentices at a time. (This rule also applied to Wheelwrights who had not served as a Master and passed the Chair. But if the latter had been fulfilled then three apprentices could be bound.)

c

The fine for failing to observe these rules was £10.

Attempts to enforce the ordinances, particularly with regard to journeymen taking up their Freedom, led to disputes and, in one case, to a petition to the Court of Aldermen—but, evidently, the petitioners were not very optimistic:

> Tuesday, 12th December, 1699
>
> Whereas upon a petition presented unto this Court on Thursday the 23 of November last by Robert Giles and other members of the Company of Wheelwrights agst the Master & Wardens & Beadle of the said Company for undue practices It was ordered that the said Petition should be signed by the Petitioners and when so signed to be delivered to the Town Clerk on the Tuesday then following in order that ye Master and Wardens might have a copy of the same And that the cause should be heard on this day Now ye sd Master and Wardens appearing and the same petition being neither signed nor delivered according to ye said order nor any of the said Petitioners now appearing it is ordered that ye said Master & Wardens be discharged from further Attendance and that the Complt of the Petitioners be rejected.

James Scott records that at the end of the seventeenth century the Company tried to keep a balance between coach-wheelers and cart-wheelers by making an order that if the Master and one Warden were coach-wheelers, the other Warden should be a cart-wheeler and vice versa; but this order was repealed after twenty years.

If the early records of the Company show that fund-raising for the corporation was difficult, it must not be assumed that the early wheelwrights were poor men.

Bartholomew Hooper, one of the original Court of Assistants and Master of the Company in 1674, who was fined for not serving as Master again in 1688, drew up his will on 24 April 1690. It is still extant and his bequests show him to have been a man of substance. They were: To his son Bartholomew, £171 10s; to his son William, £171; to his daughter Elisabeth, £171; to his daughter Anne, £171 10s. Each of the above bequests had the condition: to be paid on reaching the age of 21 or marriage, and with the consent of 'my beloved wife'. The remainder was left to his wife, and to two friends he left a golden guinea for services as executors.

When Bartholomew Hooper, Citizen and Wheelwright, died in 1691, it is clear that, considering the money values of his times, his trade had been, in the words which Campbell used half a century later, 'abundantly profitable to the Master'.

3

The Eighteenth Century:
Growth, Grandeur and Retrenchment

ONCE THE charges of incorporation had finally been paid, and
with the fines of admission to the Court of Assistants and
penalties for disobedience to the Company's bylaws increased,
the Wheelwrights entered the eighteenth century in a state of
comparative prosperity.

In 1699, the Court ordered that 'all the said Compaine's
stock in ready money shall be pute out to the best advantage
for the said Compaine's use.' James Scott records:

> The first investment was an assignment of a tally upon the Act
> of Parliament for laying an imposition on salt. A tally was a name
> given to notched sticks which, until 1783, were used for keeping
> accounts in the Exchequer, answering the double purpose of
> receipts and public records. They were inscribed on one side with
> notches, indicating the sum for which the tally was an acknow-
> ledgement, and on two opposite sides with the same sum in
> Roman characters, along with the name of the payer and the date
> of the transaction. Different kinds of notches (differing in lengths)
> stood for different values.
>
> The tally was divided, so that each piece contained one of the
> written sides and a half of each notch; one half was retained by
> the payer as his receipt, whilst the other was preserved in the
> Exchequer. The tallies and other bonds and notes were kept in the
> Company's chest, in which up to this time, the money in the
> hands of the Renter Warden had been kept. The Clerk, and some
> times the Beadle, held a power of attorney to receive moneys due
> from the Exchequer or at the Bank.
>
> Every year when the accounts were rendered the contents of the
> chest were inventoried. These consisted principally of bonds and
> notes by different members either for money owing by them or to
> be enforced in the event of their setting up in the trade. Frequently

at the end of the year, when the Renter Warden's accounts were received, an order was made to invest part of the balance. Indeed, at one time this was the rule rather than the exception. Sometimes this balance was laid out in purchasing lottery subscriptions. At another time it was all invested in South Sea Stock and Annuities.

The Company had by now assumed the traditional role of the craft guilds of the City of London: benevolent to the poor and needy; vigilant in the control of the wheelwright's trade; and assiduous in maintaining and improving its status in the City. Indeed, the 'Poor's Box', from which payments were made to widows and orphans and members of the Company who had by age or ill-health fallen on hard times, was presented to the Company in 1682 by Mr John Preston, then a Warden, who became Master in 1684.

The revenue for the 'Poor's Box' came from members' contributions on admission and voluntary subscriptions. Distribution was made quarterly, mainly to widows of members of the Company. For example in 1768 the amount paid out per quarter varied from 24s to 30s. But the Court was always ready to consider special cases. Thus, in 1771, 'Richard Smith, being by age and infirmities unable to work was reduced to extream want' it was unanimously agreed to give him a guinea. In the same year, Samuel King pleaded an 'extream low condition' and was granted a guinea and told 'not to apply again'. Throughout the records of the Company this mixture of charity and common sense is always in evidence. So again it is minuted in 1773: 'The Court being informed by Mr. Wilson that Ann Carter, widow of Hugh Carter, late Citizen and Wheelwright, was left in great distress by an expence of the illness of her late Husband, Order'd the whole money received of him by the Company should be returned to her, which amounts to £1.11.6d.'

Yet the Court, while generous to those in need, was diligent in prosecuting those who neglected to pay their dues to the Company:

At a Committee Court, May 28th, 1740
    The Committee was informed that Peter Paterson now in Execution at Newgate at the Suit of this Compa., had Moved the

Court of King's Bench in Order to his Discharge, and that the sd
Court upon hearing were pleased to Order him back again, and
recommended it to him to make his Submission to the Compa, and
a Letter of Submission directed to the Master was read in the
Words following viz:
Gentlemen,

My Long Confinement and Sever Sickness that I have endured
in this most deplorable place has given me a true Sense of my
past defaults to the good Compa that I have wilfully and obsti-
nately offended. I was yesterday brought up by a Rule of Court to
the King's Bench, in order to Receive the allowance as the Law
has provided for Prisoners in Gaol, but am deferred to the first day
of the next Term, being Friday come fortnight, but am apprehen-
sive of a relapse from being in the Air yesterday and returning to
close Confinement, That if your goodness would but permit me to
enjoy my liberty to go and work at my Trade again, I am fully
Resolved to become a New Man and to make all suitable and just
return to the Worthy Compa that is in my power to be done. Yr
Answer directed to me in this unhappy place will Direct me,

I am, Gentlemen,
Yr unhappy humble servant,
PETER PATERSON
Common side of Newgate
13th May, 1740.
To the Worthy Master, Wardens and Assistants of the Company
of Wheelers.

There is no record of the Company's reaction to the plea of
the unhappy Peter Paterson, but the Court did recognise that
there should be some relief for the humbler members of the
Company. In that same year, 1740, an Order was made ex-
cusing journeymen from payment of quarterage. For other
members quarterage was 2s 6d compared with the 'twelve
pence' laid down by the bylaws of 1714.

A measure of the Company's growing affluence can be
gauged by the increasing splendour of the Beadle's uniform:

1st October, 1767. The Beadle to be provided with a new plain
Great Coat and Breeches and Hatt and that his present coat be
converted into a close bodied one.

6th October, 1774. The Beadle to be provided with a Gold Lace
Hatt a Coat and Breeches of Cloth at twelve shillings per yard the
Hatt of Fred Barnard the Cloath of John Paley both members of
this Company.

2nd October, 1777. New suit of Cloaths for the Beadle Matth

Poole to make at 12s. a yard, Fred Barnard the Gold Laced Hatt
and Mr Worthing two shirts.

3rd October, 1782. The Beadle to have a new suit of Cloathes of
superfine cloth which is to be had of Messrs Josiah Barger a
liveryman of the Company and a Hatt of Mr Barnard of Bishops-
gate Street.

But of course the most conspicuous achievement of this century was not the clothing of the Beadle, but the clothing of the
Company. It was in 1734 that it was first proposed to apply to
the Court of Aldermen to grant the Company a Livery, but
the proposal was negatived. In the same year the fine for
admission to the Freedom was raised to one guinea, for those
who, not following the trade, wished to become Free by
redemption. However, in 1773 a petition was made to the
Court of Aldermen asking that the Wheelwrights be created a
Livery Company, on the ground that the Company contained
many substantial citizens, and it was granted on 7 December,
under these 'Limitations and Restrictions':

That the number of the Livery is not to exceed one hundred:
that no person shall be admitted to the Livery without first pro-
ducing the copy of his City Freedom; that the Company shall be
subject to the several Orders of the Court of Aldermen respecting
Livery Companies; that the Charter and Bylaws of the Company
shall be enrolled in the City; that a fee of £15 shall be payable on
admission to the Livery.

The Court of Assistants met on 23 December, 1773.

The Report of the Committee appointed the 19th day of
October last by the Court of Alderman to examine the allegations
of a petition presented the same day by this Company requesting
to be created a Livery Company And the Order of the Court of
Mayor and Aldermen dated 7th December 1773 for creating and
making the Wheelwrights a Livery Company under certain
Limitations and Restrictions was Read, as it may be seen at large in
the Book of Entry of all persons admitted to the Livery.

Then the Master, Samuel Harman, the Wardens, Thomas
Stafford and James Hawkins, eleven members of the Court of
Assistants: John Miles, William Caslake, Samuel Leaver,
Richard Wilson, John Rabbatts, Barrington Wood, Robert
Webb, Samuel Lloyd, William Caslake, junior, John Newbold,

Barnett Price and eight other members of the Company were clothed in the Livery. Of these first Liverymen, John Miles had been Master of the Company in 1748 and served again for part of 1773 after Richard Turrell had died in office; William Caslake had been Master in 1756, Samuel Leaver in 1768, Richard Wilson in 1770 and John Rabbatts in 1771; Barrington Wood served as Master in 1772 and in 1781 was appointed Beadle of the Company; James Hawkins became Master in 1775, Robert Webb in 1776, William Caslake, junior, in 1778, John Newbold in 1770 and Barnett Price in 1780. Each of the new Liverymen paid his admission fine of £15 together with fees of 10s, of which 7s 6d went to the Clerk and 2s 6d to the Beadle.

The Court also gave the Clerk power to admit on the Livery 'such Members as shall apply, provided they are of Known Good Character and imblemished Reputation', and it ordered 'that the Money Received for Livery Fines should be paid to its bankers, for the Company's use'. The Clerk was to 'have power to Draw and Invest the same in Old South Sea Annuities . . . whenever there shall be sufficient cash in hand to purchase 100 pound stock'.

Within the next six months another thirty-one members were admitted to the Livery, bringing the total to fifty-three by July 1774. The new Liverymen included Alexander Brander, who became Master of the Company in 1792 and Sheriff of London and Middlesex in 1793; and Benjamin Worthy, who served as Master in 1781.

In 1778 the Clerk was allowed ten guineas in consideration of the trouble he had taken in drawing up a petition to the Court of Aldermen for obtaining the Livery. But soon the Livery had reached the permitted number of 100 and there was a waiting list of members who desired to be admitted. So in 1792 the Clerk of the Company drew up another petition:

> To the Right Honourable the Lord Mayor, and Court of Aldermen.
> The humble Petition of the Master, Wardens and Assistants of the Art and Mistery of Wheelwrights of the City of London
> SHEWETH
> That on the 19 day of October 1773 a Petition of the Master,

Wardens, Assistants and Commonalty of the said Art and Mistery of Wheelwrights was presented to the Honourable Court, which after reciting several parts of the Charter of the said Art and Mistery, prayed that they might be allowed and constituted a Livery Company of this City, that this Honourable Court did on the same day refer the said Petition to a Committee of Aldermen, who were desired to examine the Allegations thereof, and report their opinion thereon.

That on the 7th day of December following the said Committee reported their opinion, that the prayer of the said Petition should be complied with, and this Honourable Court was pleased to approve and confirm the said Report, and the said Art and Mistery were constituted a Livery Company accordingly.

That your Petitioners beg leave to represent that the Number of Freemen of the said Company amount to upwards of nine hundred and they have repeated applications from many respectable Members to be admitted upon the cloathing of the said Company.

That your Petitioners are well informed that several Persons would have become Members of the said Company by Redemption, and that others who are entitled to their Freedom by Servitude and Patrimony, have refused to take up the same, being unwilling to become Members unless at the same time, they are permitted to take upon them the Cloathing thereof but as there is no Vacancy in the said Cloathing (being by an Order of this Honourable Court of 7th day of Decr. 1773 confined to one hundred Members) they cannot enjoy that priviledge and your Petitioners are thereby deprived of several respectable Members to the great prejudice and hurt of the said Art and Mistery.

> Your Petitioners therefore humbly pray that this Honourable Court will be pleased to take the premises into consideration, and grant an Increase to the number of the Livery of the said Art and Mistery of Wheelwrights under such Regulations and Orders for the honor and Dignity of this City, as this Honorable Court shall think fit.
>
> Signed by Order
> Cs. Montague
> Clerk.

The Court then resolved 'that the foregoing Resolutions be fairly transcribed and signed by the Clerk that he do wait upon Alexr. Brander with the same.' The Committee of Aldermen appointed 'to examine the allegations of the Petition' recited the previous Orders of the Court and the Petition in full and reported:

> Your Committee after duly considering thereof are of opinion that the complying with the prayer of their Petition will be bene-

ficial to the said Company by encouraging and promoting the
encrease of their Members and that the number of their Livery
should be encreased to One hundred and fifty and shall not at any
time exceed the same, and that the Master and Wardens of the
said Company of Wheelwrights for the time being do return
annually before the 24th day of Decr. to the Town Clerk's Office
a List of their Livery with their places of Abode. All which We
submit to this Honourable Court this 20th day of November 1792.

signed   Brass Crosby
Watkin Lewes
Nathl. Newnham
Paul Le Mesurier
Thos. Skinner
H. C. Combe

The report was read at the First Court held on Tuesday, 27
November 1792:

'Sanderson Mayor. And a motion being made and Question
put that this Court doth agree with the Committee in their
said Report the same was resolved in the Affirmative and
ordered accordingly.'

The grandeur that accompanied the growth of the Company
was not confined to the Beadle's clothing. For the Lord Mayor's
procession in 1782 the Court was told:

> Wm. Powell painter of Newgate Street proposes to emblazon
> Arms of England, Arms of City, Arms of the Company on 3
> banners, two yards square each of Rich Mantua silk fringed round
> with silk fringe with Poles and twined trunks Gilt &c compleat
> for the sum of £38. 13. 0 to be delivered on or before 8 Nov. next.
> Accepted and that he also provide 4 Jacketts and Caps for the
> Men that are to carry the said Banners. And the Master and
> Wardens to conduct the procession and necessary business for
> Lord Mayor's day.

In the following year (1783) the Wheelwright's Company
gave its first Lord Mayor to the City and 'ordered that the
Company attend Robert Peckham Esquire the Lord Mayor
Elect (he being a member of the Company) with the usual
ceremonies when he goes to be Sworn at Westminster. That
two new standards be ordered and the robemaker Mr Child
to provide Livery Gowns for two days attendance.' Robert
Peckham was elected Alderman in 1773 and was Sheriff in
1777, when the Company paid him £5 15s 6d 'for the part use

of the Company for the Barge provided for their attendance to Westminster when sworn Sheriff of London.' He was Master of the Company in 1800.

In spite of the increase in fines, the cost of clothes, banners and entertainments continued to exceed the Company's income, and there were various attempts to reduce expenditure. In October 1777 it was resolved that 'Members, not of the Livery, cannot be invited to the Dinner on account of binding or making free their Apprentices. No person in future is to dine at the first or second table without leave of the Master.' A year later it was ordered that no guests be allowed for the dinner. The situation had improved a little by 1791 when it was moved that the Master and Wardens could invite two friends each to dinner every Court Day and nine Assistants (by rotation) could invite one each. But in January 1794 affairs had reached a crisis. The Master observed that the payments of the Company considerably exceeded the receipts and called for a statement of income and expenses over the past three years: the following were produced.

	1791			1792			1793		
INCOME	£	s	d	£	s	d	£	s	d
Fees: Freemen & Apprentices	16	16	8	23	4	2	21	15	10
Quarterage – –	72	18	0	91	1	6	83	14	6
Fines – –	3	17	0	6	5	0	5	0	0
Interest on £2,700 Old South Sea Annuities at 3 per cent – –	81	0	0	81	0	0	81	0	0
Total Income – –	£174	11	8	£201	10	8	£191	10	4
EXPENDITURE	£	s	d	£	s	d	£	s	d
By Expense of Entertainment at the several Courts –	74	8	8	99	2	10	133	5	9
By the Summer Dinner	9	3	9	10	0	0	18	0	0
By the Committee Ct. Dinner – – –	13	0	1	9	19	0	10	17	8
By Lord Mayor's Day Dinner – – –	72	3	0	76	12	6	78	1	5
	£168	15	6	£195	14	4	£240	14	10

			1791			1792			1793		
			£	s	d	£	s	d	£	s	d
By Salaries:	Clerk,										
Beadle, etc.	–	–	51	4	0	54	12	8	51	4	0
Quarterly Poor	–	–	22	11	6	22	17	6	22	7	0
Casual Poor	–	–	6	11	0	1	1	0	8	6	0
Sundries	–	–	2	14	0	3	10	6	3	10	6
Total Expenditure	–		£251	16	0	£277	16	0	£325	12	4

	£	s	d
Average Income over the three years –	189	4	2
Average Expenditure – – – –	285	1	5

(There are two points of interest in these accounts: when Barrington Wood was elected Beadle on the death of James Unsworth in 1781, his salary was £11 per annum—the same as Unsworth's—but with an allowance of £3 on Court Days as compared with £1 4s previously. And in July 1792 it was resolved that the Summer Dinner be held at the Three Crowns, Stoke Newington, 'and not to exceed ten pounds', which was exactly the amount spent.)

Faced with these figures, the Court decided on a number of economy measures: it was ordered that the Court be summoned at 12 noon for one o'clock; that no members should absent themselves during the sitting; that there would be no refreshments at the expense of the Company on Court Days. Dessert on Court Days and on Lord Mayor's Day was to be discontinued and the Summer Feast dispensed with. Only Liverymen would be able to attend dinners, and of these only those who were not in arrears of quarterage.

In 1798, during the Napoleonic War, a Special Court was held to consider the propriety of discontinuing all dinners and to apply the savings to the defence of the country. It was pointed out that over the past four years expenditure had exceeded income by £114 10s 5d. It was recommended that the Summer Feast (which had apparently crept back) be dispensed with, and that only the Master and Wardens and one-third of the Assistants be allowed to invite friends. It was also ordered that on Court Days no person could dine without a ticket. The Master and Wardens hoped that this would suffice, but it was 'Resolved that during the War all Dinners except that of the Master in October be discontinued and that £100 be paid yearly into the Bank for the Defence of the Country against Invasion This is to be published in the *Morning Chronicle, The Times* and *Herald*.'

By a happy chance, some of the bills paid for the Company's Dinners in the last quarter of the eighteenth century still survive and they make fascinating reading. This is the account for Lord Mayor's Day in 1779:

The Worshipful Compy of Wheelwrights

To James Rowley *Dr.*

London Coffee House	Novr. 9th. 1779	£	s	d
Bread & Beer			11	0
Dinners		16	10	0
Wine		7	10	0
Punch		4	8	6
Brandy & Bry & Water			12	6
Negus			9	0
Cyder & Cup			10	0
Ale			11	0
Tobacco			6	0
Do. Herb			6	0
Cheese & Butter			11	0
Strong Beer			10	0
Tea, Coffee &c.		2	10	0
Suppers		2	0	0
Strong Beer			10	0
Biscuits &c.			2	6
Glass broke			5	0
		£38	2	6
Waiters and Cook		1	1	0
		£39	3	6

This bill was paid by Thomas Rowley on behalf of James Rowley, who became Master in 1784, on 10 January 1780

On 14 January 1780 the Worshipful Company of Wheelwrights was feasting again:

	£	s	d
Bread & Beer		10	0
Breakfasts		5	0
Pd. Cods head		10	0
Pd. Sallmon		9	0

	£	s	d
Pd. Whitings – – – – – – –		2	0
Pd. Smelts – – – – – – –		3	0
Pd. Lobsters – – – – – – –		2	0
Dress Fish wh Sauce &c. egg & Anchovy – –		8	0
8 Fowls & Dress wh Gravy &c. – – – – –		12	0
4 Wild Duck & Dress – – – – –		16	0
Ham & Dress – – – – – – –		18	0
Soup in the morning – – – – –		4	0
Leg pork and Dress – – – – – –		6	0
Aple Sauce – – – – – – –			6
Salladoyl Egg &c. – – – – – –		1	0
Potatoes &c. – – – – – – –		1	0
Greens & Carotts – – – – – –		4	6
Aple Pye – – – – – – –		5	0
Mince Pyes – – – – – – –		10	0
Butter – – – – – – – –		3	0
Oranges & Lemons – – – – – –		2	0
Cheese – – – – – – – –		2	0
Bread & Onion Sauce – – – – –		1	0
Wine & Punch– – – – – – –	4	3	6
Ale – – – – – – – –		7	11
Coffee Tea &c. – – – – – –		15	0
Toba – – – – – – – –		3	3
Wax candles Cash to ye Beadle &c. – – –	1	7	0
Cyder Cuppe – – – – – – –		8	0
Oysters – – – – – – – –		1	6
	£15	1	2
Punch Since the Bill – – – – – –		1	6
	£15	2	8
Servants – – – – – – –		5	0
	£15	7	8

This bill was signed by the Master, Barnett Price, and is receipted 'Recvd the contents in full' by S. Marriott, who kept the 'Paul's Head Tavern'.

The dinner on 6 April 1780 was also at the 'Paul's Head'. It was a modest affair with twenty-six dinners at 4s a head, £5 4s; £3 13s for wine; a total of £12 5s 7d. But the Summer Feast on 13 July 1780 was undoubtedly elaborate:

	£	s	d
Cold Tongue Bread Beer – – – – –		5	6
Ham & Dressing – – – – – –		15	0
Paid for Haunch Venison – – – – –	2	12	6

	£	s	d
Dressing do. & Jelly Sauce &c. – – – –		10	6
6 Fowls & Dressing &c. – – – – –	1	1	0
2 Geese & Dressing &c. – – – – –		13	0
2 Ducks & do. – – – – – – –		6	0
Beans Peas & French Beans Butter &c. – –		12	6
3 Cooling Tarts Cream'd 1 do. plain ⎫ – – 2 Rasberry Tarts ⎭	1	0	0
Custard – – – – – – – –		2	6
Greens Carrotts &c. – – – – – –		1	6
Bread & Beer – – – – – – –		6	0
Apricots Rasberries Cherrys Currants – – –		18	0
Porter & Ale – – – – – – –		13	0
Tea & Coffee – – – – – – –	1	0	0
Brandy & Water – – – – – –		5	0
Cyder – – – – – – – –	1	3	0
Arrack Punch – – – – – – –	2	10	0
5 Bottles Madeira – – – – – –	1	5	0
9 Bottles Old Port – – – – – –	1	2	6
Lisbon & Mountain – – – – – –	1	0	0
Brandy Punch – – – – – – –		9	0
Red port & Madeira Made to Negus – – –	1	12	0
Lemon & Sugar – – – – – –		3	6
Tobbacco – – – – – – –		3	6
Wax Lights – – – – – – –		1	0
	£20	11	6
Servants – – – – – – –		10	6
	£21	1	0

An interesting contrast in menus is provided by a bill to the Company from the 'Paul's Head Tavern' on 14 January 1789:

	£	s	d
Cold Eating &c. in the Morning – – –		7	6
Wine &c. in the Morning – – – – –		5	6
Bread and Beer – – – – – –		10	0
Dinners – – – – – – – –	5	8	0
Lemons and Oranges – – – – –		2	6
Ale – – – – – – – –		5	5
Wine &c. – – – – – – –	4	13	6
Tobacco – – – – – – –		4	0
Officers Dinners – – – – – –		1	6
Tea and Coffee – – – – – –	1	0	0
Brandy – – – – – – –		8	0
Lemon and Sugar – – – – – –		2	0
Butter and Cheese – – – – – –		2	6
Glasses – – – – – – –		2	0

	£	s	d
Cyder Cuppe – – – – – – –		10	0
Oranges – – – – – – – –		4	9
Portugal Grapes – – – – – –		4	6
Chesnuts – – – – – – –		3	0
Apples – – – – – – – –		4	0
Olives – – – – – – – –		2	6
Biscuits – – – – – – – –		1	0
	£14	14	2
Servant – – – – – – – –		5	0
	£14	19	2

Settled by Cash   Saml Marriott

The Company did, however, have other expenses to meet.
The detailed account for the Beadle's new uniform in October
1788 is still in existence:

	£	s	d
To making Suit Beadle – – – – –		17	0
Silk and Twist – – – – – –		3	0
Slievelinings & pocketts – – – –		2	6
4½ Supr Shalloon a 2/2 – – – –		9	9
Dimity body & Slieves – – – –		3	6
Brees linings and pocketts – – – –		4	0
Silk Garters Canvas & Stays – – – –		3	6
3½ Supr Cloth a 19/- – – – –	3	6	6
	£5	12	9

Settled July 24th, 1789   S. Howe

In addition, charges had to be met continually for standard
bearers, Livery gowns, coaches, coachmen, servants for attendance on Lord Mayor's Day; and other ceremonial occasions.
There were bills for printing summonses to the Court and to
Lord Mayor's Day, indentures, Livery lists and receipts; for having the Company's chair at the 'Paul's Head' gilt and repaired.

Yet by 1798 it was decided that the Livery gowns were unfit
to be worn. New ones were ordered for the Court days from
Mr Corrock, robemaker, at £1 11s 6d per annum. (Mr Child,
the robemaker in 1784, had been paid £11 7s and Mr Holmes,
the robemaker in 1792, £7 7s. The old Livery gowns were
given to the Beadle.

The final blow was the introduction of income tax by William

A wheelwright's shop: **A** Repairing a wheel—spokes are being drawn together to allow a new felloe (section of rim) to be fitted; **B** Fitting a new spoke—the spoke-cramp holds the spoke steady while it is driven in; **C** Morticing the hub—the spoke-set has a whale-bone feeler which is designed to touch the spoke as it is driven into the mortice hole. It acts as a guide to the angle of the spoke; **D** A wheel on the wheel-horse—ready for painting; **E** Grinding paint—with a mulling-stone on a marble slab; **F** Hub borer; **G** A broad wheel, shod with strakes, ie iron shoes which cover the joints between the felloes; **H** Bettye saw—for cutting curved pieces, eg felloes; **I** Templates or patterns for felloes of various sizes; **J** Augers for boring holes; **K** Pear-shaped bellows; **L** Cart jack for lifting a cart when repairing wheel; **M** Axle made entirely of wood

Robert Peckham, Esq, Master in 1800. He was the first member of the Wheel-wrights' Company to become Lord Mayor of London, in 1783. (Taken from a painting by William Miller, now in the Guildhall Art Gallery)

Pitt in 1799, and in that year the Clerk prepared an account showing that the Company's taxable income was £210 16s, the tax payable at 10 per cent being £21 1s 7d. Every available source of income was exploited by the Company to meet these rising expenses, and every legal means of enforcing the Company's rules was employed. Fines for 'late coming' to Court were extracted on the spot. Old ordinances such as the following were revived and confirmed.

> 28th March, 1771
> The Order of 8th January, 1735, was read: Resolved nem.con. that no Cart Wheelwright shall from and after the next Midsummer Court be admitted an Assistant of this Company without first paying to the Renter Warden for the Company's use the sum of fifteen pounds.
> Resolved, nem.con. that the said Resolution above recited be continued and confirmed in full force.

The views of members' work and workmanship, together with fines for the use of inferior materials or making 'rotten wheels', continued throughout the century:

8th July, 1773	£	s	d
Recd. of Mr. Leaver for the Whitechapel Search –	2	7	9
Recd. of Mr. Stafford for the Southwark do. –	4	6	0
Recd. of Mr. Harman for the St. Giles do. –	4	19	4

Ordered Mr. Burch and Mr. Webb be fined 5s. each for neglecting going to the search and Mr. Webb paid his fine in Court.

New fees were introduced in 1776, when it was decided to charge one guinea for binding an apprentice in Court, and for every apprentice bound out of Court £1 5s and 'that there be 2s 6d additional reserved for each and every such binding for the Company's use'. In 1784 the admission fees were raised from 10s to 15s; 10s going to the Clerk and 5s to the Beadle. Then in 1792 it was decided to pay one guinea to a person recommending a new Member, provided that 2s 6d was given for the Company's use.

Persistent attempts were made to recover fines due and payments in arrear. In 1783 William Major was fined £20 for refusing to come on the Court of Assistants. When he did not pay, the Attorney was directed to bring action for its recovery, but there is no record of the fine being recovered. In the

D

following year: 'Mr. King, Attorney, doubts if there is sufficient evidence to recover quarterage from Sam Lindley. Ordered that the Beadle take a witness with him and demand the arrears from him.' Again there is no mention of the result.

From 1795 to 1797 there was a big drive to collect arrears of quarterage. John Font, who had been Master of the Company in 1782, and whose name had long 'led all the rest' in the minute-book records of those owing quarterage was, after numerous warnings, 'hereby discharged from his place of Assistance . . . for his non-appearance and neglect' in July 1795. By October 1797 the Clerk and Beadle had collected £80 9s 6d of arrears.

There was one other way of raising funds which proved particularly profitable in the early years of the nineteenth century. In 1794 David Davidson, who had been Master of the Company in 1791, asked to be translated to the Fishmongers, so it was decided that 'if Mr. Davidson pay £50 into the Poor's Box, this Court will agree to his translation to the aforesaid Company, and upon the shew of hands the same was carried in the Negative. Motion was then made and seconded that if Mr. Davidson pay £100 into the Poor's Box, this Court will agree his translation, and upon the shew of hands the same was carried in the Affirmative.'

One interesting aspect of the Company's development in the eighteenth century was the widening, both socially and geographically, of the admissions to membership, as shown in the record of the entry of Freemen and Freewomen. For example, in 1794 Ralph Wedgwood, son of Thomas Wedgwood, Potter, late of Burslem, Stafford, was made a Freeman by Redemption; Joel Cadbury, son of Joel Cadbury of Exeter, Broker; while Jane Nairne, widow of Richard Nairne, Gent, late of Ramsgate, Kent, became a Freewoman. In 1796 the curiously named John Ogle Ogle, son of Mathew Williamson of Yorkshire, was made a Freeman; but the most delightful entry is one of 1794, when Original Hayward, son of Original Hayward, of Great Ealing, Middlesex, was bound apprentice to Edward Lloyd, Assistant, for seven years.

4

The Eighteenth Century:
Disputes and the Law

THE HISTORY of the Wheelwrights in the eighteenth century
was of course more than a record of finance and feasting. The
Company inevitably became involved in the periodical waves
of industrial unrest which spread through London and the
country. It has already been recorded that as early as 1679 the
Master, Wardens, and some of the Assistants of the Company
had been called to order for forming a combination to raise
prices. All such combinations, whether by master craftsmen or
their workmen were illegal; but in practice the Masters could,
and often did, form cartels, whereas any such action by
journeymen or workmen was usually severely dealt with both
by the Masters themselves and the magistrates. This state of
affairs continued until trade unionism was legalised, in theory
at least, in 1825.

The first brush between masters and men in the wheelwright's trade occurred in 1714, when a number of workmen
formed a Journeymen's Club. Its objects were to further the
interests of working wheelwrights, with particular attention to
wages and working conditions. At first this caused little stir,
because the men made no immediate demands; but ten years
later the Company showed its disapproval by making an order
that members of the Journeyman's Club should not be allowed
on the Court of Assistants.

In 1734 a number of the City's Journeymen Coach Wheelwrights did form an active combination to demand shorter

hours and higher wages. They threatened to strike unless their working day was reduced by two hours, and they wanted an extra shilling for every pair of hind wheels and an extra shilling for hewing every 100 spokes. The Master Wheelwrights refused the demands, claiming that they could not pay more than one guinea a week. The Company appointed a committee to consider the crisis, and while this committee was seeking counsel's opinion as to the legality of the combination, the journeymen went on strike.

In October 1734 Counsel advised the Company that in his view there was sufficient evidence of a conspiracy for the men to be charged, either under a Statute of Edward VI or at Common Law. The Company then proceeded against forty-two of the journeymen by bringing an indictment for conspiracy, and the Grand Jury returned a true bill. Counsel for the defence then suggested a basis for settlement: that the journeymen should receive an extra sixpence for every pair of hind wheels, and that the working hours should be from 5 am to 7 pm in summer and from 6 am to 8 pm in winter. The Court would not agree to this and instructed its committee to proceed with the prosecution. For some reason not stated the Company changed its mind a few months later: whether the cost of legal action or doubts about its success influenced the Court is not known, but it decided not to go on with the prosecution until further order. There was no further order and the matter dropped.

The next dispute between tradesmen and masters was more serious and widespread. It began at the end of 1781, when the Journeymen Wheelwrights of London made a solid front and demanded increased piece-work rates and a rise in day wages. When the Master Wheelwrights refused, the entire body of journeymen went on strike and held meetings to raise strike funds. The Company then had recourse to legal action and, on 18 April 1782,

> Mr WARDEN PERRYMAN informed the Court, that on or about Christmas last, the Journeyman in the trade made a general application to the Masters for advancing the price of wages from

fourteen shills to eighteen shillings per sett for making Wheels, and the day men to be raised in proportion; on the Trade in general refuseing to comply, the Journemen one an all left work, proceeded to hold meetings, & raised subscriptions for endeavouring to bring the Masters to comply with their demandes. These proceedings induced the Master Mr Font to apply for advice to the Bench of Justices, who were unanimous in the Opinion that such meetings & combinations were Illegal & that the Master might & indeed ought to indite them at the Sessions, on which Mr Font with the assistance of the Peace Officers gott possession of their subscription book, then prefered a Bill of Inditement at Hickes Hall against six or eight of the principals which by the Grand Jury was returned a Good Bill in consequence the Delinquents were taken into custody and admitted to bail, by their Council moved to have the tryal put off till the next Sessions.

THE COURT after duly considering the matter, came to the following Resolutions Viz

THAT the present wages is sufficient to enable an industrious workman to provide for himself & Family

THAT the profitts of the Trade will not allow of givin the advanced wages required

THAT the Father of the Company, having given the advanced wages, has been a means of supporting the above combinations, which is & has been a detriment to the trade in generall, therefore he has incured the censure of this Court & the Court unanimously Censure him accordingly

THAT the Court will indemnify the Master for all the expences he has or may be at in suppressing the said Combination and prosecuting the Delinquents.

The account of the preliminary proceedings still exists in the Middlesex Quarter Sessions Records for 5 February 1782, when James Ayres, William Eldridge, Jacob Freeman, Philip Holland, John Medley, George Parry and John Wilson were indicted for 'petty larceny'. They appeared before a Bench of twelve judges at Hicks Hall. The seven men,

all of the parish of St. Andrew Holborn and belonging to the Art Mistery and Manual occupation of wheelwright, not content to work and labour the usual number of hours in each day and at the usual rate and prices which they and other workmen and Journeymen in the same art and mystery and manual occupation were used wont and accustomed to work and labour. . . .

On the 29 January in the 22nd year of the reign of King George III and at the parish aforesaid in the county aforesaid unlawfully falsely and fraudulently did conspire combine confederate and agree together unlawfully unjustly and oppressively to increase and augment the wages of themselves and other Journeymen in the same art Mystery and unjustly to exact and extract great sums of money for their labour and hire in their Art and Mystery from their Masters who should employ them therein.

And the Jurors James Ayres William Eldridge Jacob Freeman Philip Holland John Medley George Parry and John Wilson together with the said divers other persons unknown on the said 29 January unlawfully did assemble and meet together and so being then and there assembled and met together then and there unlawfully unjustly and corruptly did coveneant conspire combine confederate and agree among themselves that the said James Ayres William Eldridge Jacob Freeman Philip Holland John Medley George Parry and John Wilson would not make or do any work in their said Art Mystery or Manual Occupation but at a certain extraordinary price or rate (to wit) the sum of four shillings more than usual price of fourteen shillings for the making of every set of wheels and that they the aforesaid . . . will not work or labour any longer in the said Art Mystery or Manual Occupation of Wheelwright to the evil example of all others against the peace of our said Lord the King his Crown and Dignity and also against the form of Statute in such case made and provided . . . to the great damage and oppression not only of the several Masters employing them in the same Art and Mystery but also of divers other liege subjects of our said Lord the King. . . .

On the back of the report are the names of the Master, Wardens and Assistants preferring the indictment: John Font, Thomas Perryman, Samuel Patmore, Richard Lanceloy, Thomas Ireland, James Birch, Thomas Pearson, William Major; with the words, 'Sworn in Court. True Bill.'

This was one of the last hearings to be held at Hicks's Hall, then the Sessions House of the County of Middlesex, in St John Street, Clerkenwell. It was named after Sir Baptist Hicks (afterwards Viscount Campden), a mercer of Cheapside and one of the justices of the county, at whose cost it was built in 1612. It staged many historic trials, but by 1779 it had become so dilapidated that the magistrates obtained an Act empowering them to remove their Sessions House to a more convenient site on Clerkenwell Green. It was at the first Sessions in this new Sessions House that the journeymen appeared for trial on 1 July 1782. The Master gave the Company the result on 4 July:

Mr Font informed the Court that the persons who he mentioned last Court to have a Bill of Indictment found against them at Hickes Hall for an illegall Combination had received their tryalls at the Sessions that John Wilson, Jacob Freeman, Henry Hickson, Willm Eldridge, Geo Parry, James Eyres Ar Medley were fully Convicted. Judgement had not been passed. Philip Holland was acquitted.

It is curious that Henry Hickson, who was not mentioned in the initial indictment at Hicks's Hall, should have been found guilty, but the records are incomplete. There is no mention of what sentences, if any, were given to the convicted men, who were in the custody of the Court on 1 July. It is possible that they were bound over and released.

The Company had been energetic, not only in prosecuting the striking journeymen, but in breaking the strike by importing labour from outside London. In October 1782 the Court allowed the Master £41 1s 4d paid by him to E. Jones for prosecuting their journeymen at Hicks's Hall, and also £52 17s 6d for 'various expenses in advertising for journeymen and bringing them out of the country'.

Meanwhile, the Company was also seeking legal action against wheelwrights who had not been properly indentured. In 1781 it reported: 'The Charter of the Company is to be laid before Mr. Dunning for his opinion whether the Company can prevent persons following the trade of a wheelwright not having served their apprenticeship.' Counsel was evidently of the opinion that the Company could so do, and in October 1782 the Court resolved that: 'Mr. Worthy is empowered to direct William Holden to prefer Bills of Indictment at Hickes Hall against William Austen and others for following the trade of wheelwrights not having served apprenticeship.' And the committee appointed in March 1783 'to conduct the suits' comprised Benjamin Worthy (Master in 1781), Messrs. Leaver (Master in 1768), Webb (Master 1776) and Friend (Master 1788).

There is no record of the action, but it was certainly successful, because in 1787 a motion was made at a Court of Assistants that certain members should be 'reimbursed for expenses of prosecution against journeymen working unlawfully, for which they were condemned and imprisoned.' After some debate this motion was referred to the next Court, which, on 17 October 1787, ordered that eight wheelwrights be paid £20 16s 'being their proportion of the expense of prosecuting and convicting the refractory journeymen'. The Court also moved a formal vote of thanks to the committee for their successful endeavours.

This was the last attempt by the Company to control the Trade by the legal enforcement of the provisions of the Charter and the Company's Bylaws. The changing conditions of industry in the nineteenth century and the growth of trade unionism, together with the gradual decline of craft apprenticeship, made the Company's role as arbitrator of wages and conditions superfluous. But it still had a great part to play in encouraging the Trade and in the corporate and social life of the City of London.

From the earliest times the Wheelwrights of London had had their work controlled, directly or indirectly, by the City's bylaws—which were concerned mainly with the preservation of road surfaces and not with the quality and construction of wheels.

In 1277, during the reign of Edward I, the City passed a bylaw which decreed that 'no cart serving the City, bringing water, wood, stones, etc. be shod with iron' and this law was reaffirmed in 1391. But it was clear that unshod wheels—wheels without iron strakes or tyres—could not last long, even in unpaved streets. In 1485 the Common Council banned the use of long and square-headed nails, injurious to the pavement, and ordered that all cart wheels should thenceforth be shod 'with flat nails according to the sample preserved in the Chamber of the Guildhall'.

By the middle of the eighteenth century, with carts, carriages, stage coaches and stage wagons (the heavy goods conveyances drawn by teams of eight horses at walking pace) pounding the unmade and unpaved roads into ruts of varying widths, it became necessary to make national legislation. The General Turnpike Act, 13 George III of 1773, became known as the Broad Wheels Act, because of its discrimination in favour of broad-wheeled vehicles, thought to act as steam-rollers by smoothing out the ruts. For the next forty years the width of wheels, the manner of their construction and their effects upon the roads were to become a matter of lively controversy between scientists, engineers, coachmakers and wheelwrights and Parliamentary Committees. A pamphlet written by Daniel Bourn, of Leominster, entitled *A Treatise upon Wheel Carriages &c.*, dedicated to the Society of Arts and printed in 1763, describes the origin of broad wheels:

> The first set of Broad Wheels made use of in Roads in this kingdom, were erected by Mr. James Morris of Brock-Forge, near Wigan in Lancashire, who having a deep bad road to pass with his team, advised with me upon the subject; I mentioned the making of the fellies of his Wheels of uncommon width. He accordingly made his first set 13 inches, and the next year another of nine inches in the sole; and his travelling with these to Liverpool, Warrington and other places, was took notice of by some persons of distinction, particularly Lord Strange and Mr. Hardman, Member for Liverpool &c. who, after making strict enquiries of Mr. Morris concerning their nature and properties, reported their utility to the House, which occasioned an Act of Parliament being made in their favour.

The Act of 1773 was of vital importance to the Wheelwrights of London who made road wagons and carts, because their customers, under the provisions of the new law, could pay less in tolls for broad-wheeled vehicles. This was an important consideration for those carriers and coachmasters who conveyed goods and passengers for long distances between London and provincial towns. Among the regulations made by the Act were:

> That no Carriage . . . shall pass along any Turnpike Road, being above Twenty Miles from the Cities of London or Westminster, unless the same shall be made and constructed in such Manner, that no pair of such Wheels shall be wider than Four Feet Six Inches from Inside to Inside, to be measured on the Ground, (except Wheels having the Soles of the Fellies thereof of the Breadth of Nine Inches, which shall be so constructed as to roll a Surface of Sixteen Inches; and the wider Pair of such Wheels shall

not be more than Five Feet Eight Inches from Inside to Inside, to be measured on the Ground), and that the Distance from the Centre of Fore Wheel to the Centre of the Hind Wheel of any Waggon or Four-Wheeled Carriage, not being used for the Carriage of Timber only, be not above Nine Feet, to be measured from the Centre of the Axle-trees at the Ends thereof, on Pain of the Owner or Owners of every such Waggon, Wain or Cart, forfeiting the Sum of Five Pounds for every such Offence: And the Surveyor or Surveyors, Gate-Keeper or Gate-Keepers, of any Turnpike Roads, is and are hereby authorised and required, at any Turnpike or Toll-gate, or at any other Place upon the Turnpike Road, to measure every such Waggon, Wain, or Cart; and if any Master or Driver of any Waggon, Wain, or Cart, shall hinder, or refuse to permit such Surveyor or Surveyors, Gate-keeper, or Gate-keepers, to measure such Waggon, Wain, or Cart, as aforesaid, he or she shall forfeit the Sum of Five Pounds; and it shall not be lawful for any such Waggon, Wain, or Cart, not permitted to be measured as aforesaid, to pass along any Turnpike Road.

And be it further enacted, That no Waggon, Wain or other Four-wheeled Carriage, having the Sole or Bottom of the Fellies of the Wheels of the Breadth or Gauge of Nine Inches, shall pass or be drawn on any Turnpike Road with more than Eight Horses; nor any Cart, or other Two-wheeled Carriage, having Wheels of the Breadth aforesaid, shall pass or be drawn upon any Turnpike Road with more than Five Horses; and that the Horses of such respective Carriages shall draw in Pairs; (except an odd Horse in any Team, and except where the Number of Horses shall not exceed Four); and also that no Waggon, Wain, or other Four-wheeled Carriage, having the Sole or Bottom of the Fellies of the Wheels of the Breadth of Six Inches, shall pass or be drawn on any Turnpike Road with more than Six Horses; and that no Cart, or other Two-wheeled Carriage, having Wheels of the Breadth last mentioned, shall be drawn on any Turnpike Road with more than Four Horses; and also, that no Waggon, Wain, or other Four-wheeled Carriage, having the Fellies of the Wheels of less Breadth than Six Inches, shall pass or be drawn on any Turnpike Road with more than Four Horses; and that no Cart, or other Two-wheeled Carriage, having the Fellies of the Wheels of less Breadth than Six Inches, shall pass or be drawn on any Turnpike Road with more than Three Horses; and the Owner of every such Waggon, Wain, Cart, or Carriage, shall forfeit the Sum of Five Pounds; and the Driver thereof, not being the Owner, the Sum of Twenty Shillings, for every Offence against the Provisions aforesaid, to any Person or Persons who shall sue for the same.

Provided always, That all Carriages moving upon Rollers of the Breadth of Sixteen Inches on each side thereof, with flat Surfaces, are hereby allowed to be drawn with any Number of Horses, or other Cattle. . . .

And be it enacted, That if it shall appear to the Trustees of any Turnpike Road, or any Seven of them, at any of their publick Meetings, by the Oath of One or more Witness or Witnesses experienced in Levelling, that any Part of the Rise of any Hill upon such Turnpike Road shall be more than Four Inches in a Yard; in such Case it shall and may be lawful to and for the said Trustees, or any Seven of them, to allow such Number of Horses as they shall judge necessary, not exceeding Ten for Waggons with Nine Inch Wheels, nor Six for Carts with Nine Inch Wheels; and not exceeding Seven for Waggons with Six Inch Wheels, and Five for Carts with Six Inch Wheels; and not exceeding Five for Waggons with Wheels of less Breadth than Six Inches, nor Four for Carts with Wheels of less Breadth than Six Inches: and in case it shall appear to the said Trustees, in Manner aforesaid, that the whole Rise of any Hill taken together shall be more than Four Inches in a Yard upon an Average, it shall and may be lawful for the said Trustees, or any Seven of them, to allow such Number of Horses as they shall think fit to be used in such Waggons and Carts respectively, for the Purpose only of drawing the same up such Hill or Hills to be specified in such Order of Allowance, and the Termination at each End thereof to be marked by a Post or Stone, to be erected at such respective Boundaries. . . .

And whereas great Damage is done to Turnpike Roads by Waggons, and other Carriages, with narrow Wheels, drawn by Horses in Pairs; for Remedy thereof, be it enacted, That it shall not be lawful for any Waggon, Wain, or Cart, having the Sole or Bottom of the Fellies of the Wheels thereof of less Breadth or Guage than Nine Inches, to pass upon any Turnpike Road, or through any Turnpike Gate or Bar, if the same be drawn by Horses in Pairs, (other than and except such Waggons, Wains, or Carts, having the Fellies of the Wheels thereof of the Breadth of Six Inches, as shall be authorised to be drawn in any other Manner by Order of the Trustees of any Turnpike Road within their District, made at a publick Meeting, consisting of Seven Trustees, or more; which Order it shall and may be lawful for the said Trustees to revoke at any subsequent Meeting, and afterwards to make a new One, if they shall think fit, for the same Purpose, and fixed in Writing upon every Toll-gate within such District, and except Carriages drawn by Two Horses only).

Offenders against these directions could be apprehended by any constable, tythingman, surveyor, or any other person, and upon conviction were liable to a fine not exceeding five pounds and not less than ten shillings.

And whereas in and by several Acts of Parliament, made for amending and repairing particular Turnpike Roads, several high and extraordinary Tolls are granted, and directed to be levied and paid for Waggons, Carts, and other Carriages, drawn by more than a certain Number of Horses, or Beasts of Draught, therein respectively mentioned, with an Intent, in Effect, to prohibit the Passage of such Carriages, and thereby the better to preserve the said Roads; now it is hereby further enacted, That it shall and may be lawful to and for the said Trustees appointed, or to be appointed, in or by virtue of any Act of Parliament made for repairing and amending such particular Roads, as aforesaid, or any Five or more of such Trustees respectively, within their respective Districts, and they are hereby authorised and required, at the First Meeting after the Commencement of this Act, to mitigate, lessen, and reduce the said high and extraordinary Tolls and Duties, for and in respect of such Waggons, or other wheeled Carriages only, having the Wheels of the Breadth or Gauge of Six Inches, as aforesaid, in such Manner as no greater Toll or Duty, in respect to Waggons, be demanded or taken for the same than is provided and directed by the said Acts respectively to be paid and taken for Waggons, and other Four-wheeled Carriages, drawn by Four Horses, or Beasts of Draught; and that no greater Toll or Duty be demanded or taken for Carts, having the Fellies of their Wheels of the Breadth or Gauge of Six Inches, than is provided and directed by such Acts respectively to be taken for Carts drawn by Three Horses; and the said Trustees, within their respective Districts, or any Five or more of them respectively, are hereby authorised and required to give Directions, in Writing, to the several Collectors within such their respective Districts, to take and receive such Tolls and Duties, and no other; any Law or Statute to the Contrary notwithstanding.

And be it further enacted, That the Trustees appointed by virtue or under the Authority of any Act of Parliament, made for repairing or amending Turnpike Roads, or such Person or Persons as are authorised by them, shall and may, and are hereby required, to demand and take, for every Waggon, Wain, Cart, or Carriage, having the Fellies of the Wheels thereof of less Breadth or Guage than Six Inches from Side to Side at the least, at the Bottom or Sole thereof, and for the Horses or Beasts of Draught, drawing the same, One Half more than the Tolls or Duties which are or shall be payable for the same respectively; and for every Waggon, Wain, Cart, or Carriage, having the Fellies of the Wheels thereof of less Breadth or Gauge than Six Inches from Side to Side, at the least, at the Bottom or Sole thereof, and for the Horses, or Beasts of Draught, drawing the same, from and after the Twenty-ninth Day of September, One thousand seven hundred and seventy-six, Double the Tolls or Duties which are or shall be payable for the same respectively, by any Act or Acts of Parliament made for amending or repairing Turnpike Roads, before any such Waggon, Wain, Cart, or Carriage respectively, shall be permitted to pass through any Turnpike Gate or Gates, Bar or Bars, where Tolls shall be payable by virtue of any such Acts.

And whereas there are in several Acts of Parliament for making, amending, and repairing Turnpike Roads, Exemptions allowed from Payment of Tolls in particular Cases therein respectively mentioned, and Liberties are allowed in particular Cases to pay less Tolls than are charged upon other Waggons, Wains, Carts, and Carriages, passing through Turnpike Gates or Bars: and whereas it will tend to the Advantage and Preservation of Turnpike Roads to confine such Exemptions, Liberties, Privileges, and Advantages, to Carriages with Wheels of the Breadth or Gauge of Six Inches or upwards; be it therefore enacted, That no Person shall, by virtue of the said Acts of Parliament, have claim, or take the Benefit or Advantage of any Exemption from Toll, or Part of Tolls, or to pay less Toll for or in respect of any Waggon, Wain, Cart, or other Carriage, or Horse drawing the same, and carrying any particular Kind of Goods, than other Carriages of the like Nature, carrying other Goods, ought to pay, unless such Waggon, Wain, Cart or other Carriages have the Sole of the Bottom of the Fellies of the Wheels thereof of the Breadth or Gauge of Six Inches, or upwards . . . but that the Toll required by the said Acts respectively, together with the additional Tolls hereby required to be taken for or in respect of every such Waggon, Wain, Cart, or other Carriage, having the Sole or Bottom of the Fellies of the Wheels thereof of less Breadth or Gauge than Six Inches, as aforesaid, and for and in respect of Horses, or Beasts of Draught, drawing the same . . . shall be paid the same Manner, to all Intents and Purposes, as if no Exemption, or less Toll, had been enacted or allowed by any of the said Acts respectively, and as fully as all other Waggons, Wains, Carts, and Carriages, and Horses drawing the same, ought respectively to pay, which are not intitled to any Exemption from Toll, the Whole or Part; or to pay a less Toll than other Waggons, Wains, Carts, and Carriages; any Law or Statute to the Contrary notwithstanding.

Provided, That no Person or Persons be allowed to take the Benefit of any such Exemptions, or to have the Privilege hereinbefore given of compounding in respect of any Carriage having the Fellies of the Wheels thereof of the Breadth or Gauge of Six Inches, or upwards, unless the Fellies, and the Tire upon such Fellies, shall lie flat.

Provided also, That all Waggons, Carts, or Carriages, moving upon Rollers, of the Breadth of Sixteen Inches on each Side thereof, with flat Surfaces, shall be permitted to pass or be drawn upon any Turnpike Road Toll-free, for the Term of One Year, to be computed from Michaelmas, One thousand seven hundred and seventy-three; and from and after the Expiration of the said Term, all such Waggons, Carts, or Carriages, as aforesaid, shall pass upon any Turnpike Road, through any Toll-gate or Bar, upon paying only so much of the Tolls and Duties as shall not exceed One Half of the full Toll or Duty payable by this or any other Turnpike Act, for all Waggons, Wains, or Carts, having the Fellies of the Wheels of the Breadth or Gauge of Six Inches from Side to Side, or for the Horse or Beasts of Draught drawing the same, and not rolling a Surface of Sixteen Inches on each Side thereof; and that no more than Half Toll shall be paid in respect of Waggons having the Fellies of the Wheels thereof of the Breadth of Nine Inches, and rolling a Surface of Sixteen Inches on each Side thereof, from and after the Commencement of this Act; any Thing herein contained to the Contrary notwithstanding.

Provided always, That nothing herein-before contained shall extend, or be construed to extend, to any Chaise-marine, Coach, Landau, Berlin, Chariot, Chaise, Chair, Calash, or Hearse, or to the Carriage of such Ammunition or Artillery as shall be for His Majesty's Service, or to any Cart or Carriage drawn by One Horse, or Two Oxen, and no more; or to any Carriage, having the Sole or Bottom of the Fellies of the Wheels thereof of the Breadth of Nine Inches, which shall be laden with One Block of Stone, One Piece of Marble, One Cable Rope, One Piece of Metal, or One Piece of Timber.

This last proviso put the coachmakers in a favoured position, for they could provide wheels of any width they chose for the carriage trade; the wheelwrights, as builders of commercial wagons and carts, were obviously affected by the new law. (For the interpretation of the vehicles exempted, a chaise was a light open carriage for one or two persons, with a folding hood; a chaise-marine was a kind of chaise, the body of which rested on suspension-straps between cee-springs; a chair was a light chaise, drawn by one horse; a chariot was a light four-wheeled carriage with only back seats; a calash was a light carriage with low wheels, having a removable folding hood; a landau was a four-wheeled carriage with a sunshine roof; and a berlin was a four-wheeled covered carriage, with a seat behind covered with a hood.)

The Broad Wheels Act soon caused controversy in the Trade, and many wagoners complained that the additional exertion of moving heavy wagons with broad wheels was ruining their horses. Now the scientists and theorists began to examine the wheelwright's traditional craft.

The first of them was Alexander Cumming, FRS, a mathematician and mechanic, born in Edinburgh in 1733. He came to London and set up as a successful watchmaker in Bond Street and on his retirement moved to Pentonville, where he engaged in a number of scientific experiments. In 1796 he appeared before a Parliamentary Committee, to which he explained that the damaging effects of wagon wheels on the roads were caused by the dishing of the wheels. Dished wheels he called conical wheels, because they resembled an inverted cone. Cumming advocated cylindrical wheels, that is wheels in which the spokes were either straight or dished alternately, so that the wheel was always upright and the nave always at right-angles to the axletree.

In 1797 he published *Observations on the Effects which Carriage Wheels with Rims of Different Shapes have on the Roads*, and in 1804 a fuller study on *The Destructive Effects of the Conical Broad Wheels of Carriages controverted; with the improving Effects of Cylindrical Wheels of the same breadth, as they regard the roads, the labour of cattle, etc.*

> At his house in Pentonville, Cumming 'prepared an apparatus for illustrating and corroborating, by experiment, every conclusion he had drawn from his theory: and having exhibited his experiments to Trustees; to persons extensively concerned in the Waggon trade; to Farmers; to Wheelers; and to such others as they chose to introduce, they have without exception declared, That they never had the most distant idea of true *cause* of that resistance which they had uniformly experienced with the Broad Wheel; that they had always conceived it to depend wholly on the breadth and flat bearing of the Wheel, and that it was inseparable from the flat bearing of the whole breadth, whatever might be the shape:— That they were now perfectly satisfied that the resistance arose from *the conical shape*:—That the breadth of the Cylindrical Wheel *might* be increased without increasing the resistance to its progress: —And finally, That the Conical Wheel is very destructive to the Roads, and unfavourable to the Cattle: And that all the properties of the Cylindrical Wheel are of the most favourable nature to both: And they not only made this candid and voluntary declaration, *but have given it under their hands, for the satisfaction of others.*'

This was part of Alexander Cumming's evidence submitted to the Parliamentary Committee on the Highways of the Kingdom, which published three reports as White Papers between 1806 and 1808.

Mr A. Walker, of Hayes, Middlesex, Lecturer in Mechanical Philosophy, in his evidence to the Committee agreed with Mr Cumming in theory, but not in practice. In a long paper, illustrated with diagrams, he pointed out:

> Wheels and their Axles were formerly all of one piece, as in the Irish Car and the Peat Carts of Westmoreland. Wheels fixed perpendicularly to their Axles is a very natural union; the whole went round together; and though inconvenient in turning, it is a question whether we have improved this primitive Wheel and Axle. Greater loads increasing with greater trade, room in Carriages became an object. Dished Wheels were contrived, which gave room for the body of the Carriage and set it upon a broader base, less liable to be overturned; for the underpart of the Axle being horizontal, and the upper inclined downwards from the hilt, made it stronger, and put the Wheel into this position when in action; the lowest spoke standing always perpendicular to the load, and the highest guarding it from the infraction of tumultuous Carriages or the motions of its own body. But its greatest advantage is the stiffness with which it resists lateral or sideway obstructions, those insidious inclined ruts that break Wheels imperceptibly.
>
> But the want of room still increasing, the ends of the Axle were bent downwards as a remedy, as well as for the purpose of strength; for as a Wheel is but a circular prop, the more perpendicular it stands under its load the better it sustains it, and therefore the dished Wheel may be said to exert a power in proportion to the weight that is thrown upon it.
>
> In crowded assemblies, where Coaches are every moment running foul of each other, they would tear each other to pieces if the Axles were to encounter; but as the highest part of a Wheel projects over its Axle, the bending of that axle suffers the tops of the Wheels to rub each other in passing without further mischief. In travelling on the sides of roads swelling in the middle, Carriages would overset if it was not for the broad foundation on which Dished Wheels place them; besides, in such Roads the load is thrown on the outside Wheels, and would be liable to break them if the spokes did not stand upright in a sloping situation.
>
> The double Dished Wheel with alternate spokes, I brought up to Town thirty years ago, and it may be supposed to have my particular approbation. Certainly for strength it exceeds all others, and is therefore principally made use of for Mail and Stage Coaches and other low-wheeled Carriages carrying great loads; but as its axle ought to be straight, it is unfit for Town or crowded Roads.

The only wheelwright to give evidence before the Parlia-

Some of the Company's plate

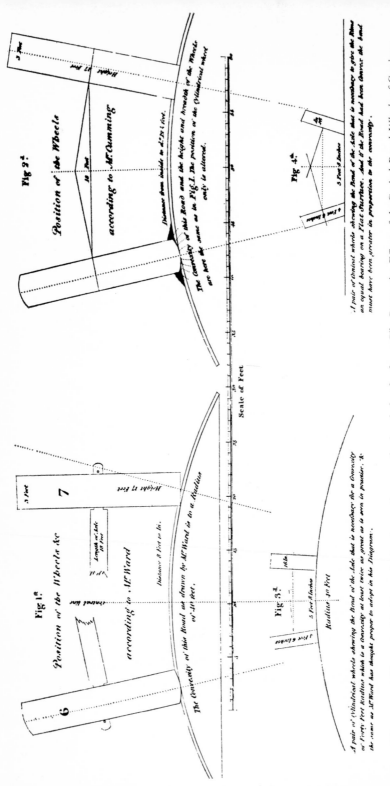

Diagrams to illustrate Mr Cumming's observations on the bended axle, from *The Destructive Effects of the Conical Broad Wheels of Carriages controverted; with the improving Effects of Cylindrical Wheels of the same breadth &c* 1804, which was subsequently submitted to the Parliamentary Committee on the Highways of the Kingdom as a White Paper in 1808 mentary Committee was Mr Benjamin Worthy—not the Benjamin Worthy who was Master of the Company in 1781, but probably his son. According to a minute of 30 September 1784: 'Mr. Worthy attended the Court and desired to be admitted a Member, whereon the Court informed him that at any time when the Joiners Company would translate him, they would be ready to receive him.' On 13 January 1785 Benjamin Worthy was admitted and sworn a Freeman by Redemption and in January 1794 he was admitted on the Livery. Two years later (6 October 1796) his son was apprenticed to him: 'Benjamin Worthy, son of Benjamin Worthy, of Old Street, Wheelwright, was bound apprentice to his said father for seven years and paid 5s.'

Whether Benjamin Worthy had been one of the Wheelers who had viewed Alexander Cumming's experiments is not known, but he was certainly in favour of the new ideas:

The Evidence of Mr. BENJAMIN WORTHY, Wheelwright, of Old-street Road.

HAVE you ever made any Cylindrical Wheels?
Yes, I have made some, but not perfectly upright, nor flat in the tire. Wheels made for small Carts, are more upright, than those for heavy burthens.

What is the reason for that?
They are thought more convenient than when they are dished, for at least small Carts; when the Axle-tree is not hollow or bent, the Wheels will follow easier.

Will there be any difference of expense between the Cylindrical and Conical Wheels?
No, and the trouble of making them would be nearly the same.

Which will require the most repair, and which will wear the longest?
The Cylindrical will wear the longest, and require the least repair.

Have you ever made single Horse Carts?
Yes.

Do you think the greatest quantity of goods could be conveyed by them, or by large Waggons with the same number of Horses?
I think by single Horse Carts, but cannot ascertain the proportion.

E

Would the use of single Horse Carts be more inconvenient to the public than large Waggons, in the metropolis and its neighbourhood?

I think less than large Waggons, not being so cumbersome as they are in narrow streets.

Do you know of any advantage, arising from the practice of placing the Wheels of the Waggons or Carts, constructed for the Carriage of heavy burthens, in a position diverging from a perpendicular?

Not any, it is done to accommodate them to a broader Cart or Waggon, but does not add to their strength.

Does any reason occur to you, why the Cylindrical Wheel, standing upright on straight axles, should not be universally adopted, instead of Wheels set on bent axles, diverging from each other at the top, and having their rims therefore of a conical shape?

If they were general, I think they would be of general utility to the Roads, provided the Roads were not so round as they now are.

Do you think, in the present state of the Roads, they would be equally so?

Yes, equally advantageous.

Would the Roads become flatter, if Cylindrical Wheels were in use?

Yes, I think they would.

Do you think, if the nails were driven in the ordinary way, they would hold the tire equally fast, as rose-headed nails commonly in use, and for an equal length of time?

I think the rose-headed nails would secure the tire better in the first instance, and be more durable.

Do you think, if the Cylindrical Wheels were partially adopted, they would be advantageous to the Roads and the carrier?

Yes, they would, in proportion to the adoption.

Mr William Deacon, a wagoner of Islington, attended the Committee and brought two Wheels for their inspection: 'one a wagon wheel of nine inches, repaired in the conical form, with three rows of tires, eight streaks and rose-headed nails, eight of which were in each streak, making in the whole 120 nails in that wheel; the other wheel had been formerly of a conical shape, having new cylindrical fellies, instead of conical, put on; the tire was one solid plate nine inches broad, and of the usual length with the other tire; each tire was fastened by six counter-sunk screw-bolts and nuts within, and there were also six nails countersunk in each tire, making in the whole, screws and bolts together, only 60.' Mr Deacon contended that his experience had shown that wheels made on this principle would require less timber and much less iron, and would last much longer. He could see no difficulty in converting old conical wheels into cylindrical: the axles would need alteration but the same iron could be used with a small addition. While the same nave and spokes would do, the fellies would have to be new.

Benjamin Worthy was then re-examined:

Answers by Mr. WORTHY, an eminent Wheelwright, regarding the Expence of converting old Conical into Cylindrical Wheels.
1. WHAT do you charge Mr. Deacon, for putting on new Cylindrical Fellies on old Conical Wheels?

	£	s	d
Answer: Six new spokes and 22 fellies – –	8	1	6
Repairing and putting in the rivets – – –	1	13	0
Setting on the tire with bolts – – – –	2	3	4
Four new arms 3½ inches – – – –	8	0	0
Four long boxes and four bushes – – –	1	3	4
New bed, and fixing the arms – – – –	1	10	0
Linch-pins-bolts and washers – – – –	1	1	0
Pamling the wheels and putting in the boxes –	1	10	0
	£25	2	2

2. Is that amount the same as the expence would probably be, were you to do the same work to Conical Wheels?
Answer: Six shillings more on account of screw-bolts being more trouble in the first instance than putting in nails.
3. What is the weight of a set of arms or axles, with bolts &c. for a nine-inch Waggon, the axle being 3½ inches thick, and the Wheels Conical; and what is the weight of the same for Cylindrical Wheels on the principle on which Mr. Deacon's were made? And what do you charge per pound for iron and workmanship, also for the beds of each? And what is the usual weight of a tire for a set of nine-inch Conical Wheels, the middle tire one inch, the outer half an inch thick?

	C.	qr.	lb.	d.
Answer:—Nine-inch axle with bolts for Four Wheels – – – – – – –	2	1	8	8
Set of boxes for do. – – – – –	1	0	0	3

Cylindrical axles and boxes full half a hundredweight less for a set.

	£	s	d
The tire of nine-inch Conical Wheels with nails is	12	2	0
Do. for Cylindrical do. do. – – – –	9	2	0

Difference in favour of the Cylindrical   –   –   £3   0   0
Conical tire, inch thick in the middle, and ⅜ outsides
Cylindrical, half an inch thick and all in one width.

4. What difference do you suppose there would be in the weight of the beds and fellies of four nine-inch Conical Wheels, and four nine-inch Cylindrical Wheels; and do you not suppose that if Cylindrical Wheels were general, they would ultimately require less wood, and less labour, than the present Conical Wheels?

Answer:—The weight of beds nearly the same; but, as the fellies of the Cylindrical Wheels may be made thinner, if of solid width of tire, they will of course be much lighter than Conical. Less wood, and less labour, would of course be needful with Cylindrical Wheels.

5. Do you not suppose, that in the event of Cylindrical Wheels becoming general, that less iron would be needful for the first tire, and that less labour would be requisite to make it, and less trouble in putting it on? And do you suppose the consumption of iron, or wear of the same, on Cylindrical Wheels, would be much less than now is on Conical Wheels? And also, that the wear of horizontal axles would be less than the present axles used for Conical Wheels?

Answer:—Less iron, as before stated, less labour in making the tire, but little difference in putting it on, as before stated.

The general consumption of iron with Cylindrical Wheels would, no doubt, be much less than now is with Conical Wheels; the wear also of the axles would be less, as less friction would be found.

It is interesting to compare these costings, as charged to the client, with the piece-work rates of the journeymen who struck for higher wages only a quarter of a century before.

The controversy about the shapes of wheels and the need for amending legislation to the Broad Wheels Act went on, in and out of Parliament. But the advent of railways and the gradual decline of the stage coach, the stage wagon and the turnpike roads solved that problem. The wheelwright's trade was changing; meanwhile the Worshipful Company of Wheelwrights of London was not only changing but growing at the same time.

5

The Nineteenth Century: Diversification

THE WHEELWRIGHTS began the nineteenth century with their familiar switchback ride from affluence to financial difficulty. In 1800 it was resolved that dinners would be provided on Court Days, but that guests, except those of the Master and Wardens, would have to pay 10s 6d.

In 1801 the Clerk testified, on a tax return form for the Company, that their income did not exceed £172 and that he was willing to pay £10 15s. In 1802 two assistants were appointed to the Beadle for the collection of quarterage and the Dinner on Lord Mayor's Day was dispensed with.

The year 1803 brought a windfall, when Sir William Leighton, Knight and Alderman and Sheriff Elect, asked to be translated from the Wheelwright's Company to the Fishmongers and proposed to pay £200 for the privilege. The Court agreed and decided that the money should be invested in Old South Sea Annuities and that the interest should be used for the poor. And it was soon put to such good use:

> 4th October, 1804
> Upon humble petition of Richard Friend, late one of the Court of this Company, praying relief on account of his great distress &c. it is ordered that he be paid the sum of £3, being the first half year's interest on £200 Old South Sea Annuities purchased by order of the Court the 15th September 1803 with the money arising from the sum paid by Sir William Leighton for his translation.

Richard Friend had been Master of the Company in 1788. He was the first of a number of those who had fallen on hard times to benefit from Sir William Leighton's money.

In October 1804 it was also decided:

> That a Dinner be provided for the Livery on Lord Mayor's Day under the direction of the Master and Wardens on the following plan: At 6s. per head, bread and beer included; to cover the table with 50 bottles of wine; to give each gentleman a bottle of wine ticket, and that no dessert, tea or supper be introduced.

On 16 January 1806 the Court met 'instead of on January 8th, the usual Court day, deferred on account of the Funeral of Lord Nelson'. And four years later, in November 1810, the Court ordered that the 'Lord Mayor's Day Dinner be countermanded in consequence of indisposition of His Majesty and decease of Princess Amelia'.

It was reported to the Court in January 1807 'that the present Chest of the Company is so unnecessarily large it cannot conveniently be placed in any part of Guildhall. Resolved to take it to pieces and reduce it to a size when it can be placed on the ground floor of the hall.' In October 1809 the Court was told that 'John Smith, the present Master, has repaired the Company's Chest and Box and declines to be remunerated'. The Court thereupon ordered an inscription to be placed on the box.

For some time it had been noticeable that there were few wheelwrights practising the trade among the Livery, and this was still more apparent when an increase in the Livery was granted. The Clerk had drawn up a petition asking the Court of Aldermen for an increase in the Livery to 250 in 1803, but it was not until another petition was presented in 1817 that the increase was granted. The Report to the Court of Aldermen and its resolution was read and entered in the Company's minute book on 4 November 1817.

> To the Right Honourable the Lord Mayor and Court of Aldermen
>
> In obedience to an order of this Honorable Court of the 8th of October 1817, we whose Names are hereunto subscribed being appointed (amongst others) to examine the allegations in the petition of the Master Wardens and Assistants of the Art & Mistery of Wheelwrights of the City of London praying a further increase to the number of their Livery, and to report our opinion

thereon to this Court, Do humbly certify that we have accordingly
met and examined the allegations of their said petition, and do find
that on the *19th of October 1773*, a petition of the Master Wardens
and Commonalty of the said Art and Mistery of Wheelwrights was
presented to this Court, which, after reciting several parts of the
Charter of the said Art and Mistery prayed that they might be
allowed and constituted a Livery Company of this City, That this
Court did on the same day refer the said Petition to a Committee to
examine the allegations thereof and to report their opinion, That
on the 7th. of December following this Court did approve & confirm the report of the said Committee, and did order that they
should be created and made a Livery Company of this City, and
that the said Livery should granted to them under the qualifica-
tions and conditions following (that is to say) that their Livery fine
should be set at the sum of *Fifteen Pounds sterling*, that the number
of their Livery shall be subject to the several orders of this Court
respecting Livery Companies, that no member of this Company
who is of the Cloathing of any other Company of this City shall be
called on the Livery of their Company before he be translated from
such other Company openly in the Court according to the ancient
custom of this City, that they be enjoined on a Constant attendance upon the Lord Mayor for the time being on all public
occasions, and that their Charter and Bye Laws should be enrolled
among the records of this Court, and we do further find that on the
16th of October 1792, a petition from the said Master Wardens and
Commonalty of the said Art & Mistery of Wheelwrights, was
presented to this Court praying an increase of the number of their
Livery, That this Court did on the same day refer the said Petition
to a Committee to examine the allegations thereof and to report
their opinion thereon, That on the 27th day of November following this Court did approve and confirm the report of the said Committee and did order that the number of their Livery should be
encreased *to one hundred and Fifty*, and should not at any time exceed the same, It further appears to your Committee that they
have had repeated applications from respectable Members to be
admitted upon the Cloathing of the said Company, but as there
is no vacancy in the Livery the number being limited to one
hundred and fifty as aforesaid, they conceived themselves to be
deprived of several very respectable Members, Your Committee
therefore after duly considering thereof are of opinion that the
complying with the prayer of their petition will be beneficial to the
said Company by encouraging and promoting the encrease of their
Members and that the number of the Livery should be encreased
to Two Hundred and shall not at any time exceed the same, and
that the Fine should be set at the Sum of Twenty one Pounds
Sterling, that is to say, Twenty Pounds for the Company, fifteen
Shillings for the Clerk, and five Shillings for the Beadle, and that
the Master and Wardens of the said Company of Wheelwrights

for the time being, do return annually on or before the 24th day of December to the Town Clerks Office, a List of their Livery with their places of abode, all which we submit to this Honorable Court, this 10th day of October 1817.

(Signed) Richd Carr Glyn
J: J: Smith
Wm. Domville

Which report was well liked and approved by this Court, except that the number of the encrease of Livery be extended to One Hundred instead of Fifty, making in the Whole Two Hundred and Fifty Liverymen of the said Company of Wheelwrights and no more, and it is hereby Ordered that the number of the Livery of the said Company of Wheelwrights be encreased to *Two Hundred and Fifty*, and do not at any time exceed the same, and that the Fine be set at the sum of *Twenty one Pounds Sterling*, that is to say Twenty Pounds for the Company, fifteen Shillings for the Clerk, and five Shillings for the Beadle, and the Master and Wardens of the said Company for the time being are hereby required to return annually on or before the 24th. day of December to the Town Clerks office, a correct list of their Livery with their places of abode.

Signed   Woodthorpe

Resolved

That the following persons (having been nominated in the Court) be admitted on the Livery

Mr. Charles Martin, Joiner
,, John Barrow, Broker
,, John West, Cornfactor
,, John Coleby, Linen Draper
,, Thomas Stevens, Haberdasher
,, George Wright, Linen Draper
,, Edward Conder, Grocer
,, Henry Joseph Bowden, Broker
,, Stephen Cleasby, Broker
,, Joseph Rutter, Umbrella Maker
,, Joshua Stansfield Hutchinson, Stock Broker
,, George Morris, Chemist
,, John Dixon Hancock, Coachmaker
,, Charles Herring, Ship Owner
,, Christopher Richardson, ditto
,, John James Short, Broker
,, James Gould, Fishmonger
,, Francis Ceal, Tobacconist
,, Richard Gibson, Grocer
,, Samuel Williamson, Pawnbroker
,, William Norris, Stockbroker
,, Edward Knightley, Orange merchant
,, William Leedham, jun., Cheesemonger

Mr. Joseph Spratt, Warehouseman
„ Anthony Nelson, Wholesale Linen Draper
„ Jonathan Crocker, ditto
„ Alexander Milne, Pawnbroker

At the same time the Court ordered that '£25 be paid Henry Woodthorpe, Esq., Town Clerk, that there be given his principal Clerk £15 and to other clerks in his office £10 in discharge of their Fees and in compensation for their trouble in the application of the Company to the Court of Aldermen for an increase in Livery'.

It is remarkable that, even at a time when the wheelwright's craft was still of vital importance to the City and the nation, not one of the new Liverymen practised the Trade. The Wheelwrights were experiencing a diversification of membership in common with many other Livery Companies of London, whose crafts were either in decline or had ceased to be under their control. But the Wheelwright's Company did not become wholly indifferent to the Trade and, as will be seen later, continued to spend what money they could spare in training and encouraging young wheelwrights.

In the meantime the Company was growing in social prestige. On 20 October 1819 it was reported to the Court that Alderman George Bridges, who had been elected Upper Warden earlier that month, had been returned to serve as Lord Mayor for the ensuing year. He was therefore excused office, both as Warden and Master, and the Master and Wardens were requested to make the necessary arrangements to attend the Lord Mayor elect. They decided that the Beadle should have a 'new Blue Gown forthwith'; and in due course they reported to the Court on the ceremonies attended:

> Agreeably to the resolution of the Court of the 20th. of October last 'That it be referred to the Master and Wardens of the Company to make the necessary arrangements for attending George Bridges Esquire & Alderman Lord Mayor Elect, on the 8th. & 9th. days of November' We proceeded in pursuance of such reference to adopt such measures as we were of opinion were best calculated to evince the respect entertained by the Company for the Lord Mayor (one of the Members of the Court of Assistants) in attending him on his entering on that high and important office,

and also to maintain the respectability of the Company in the public procession connected therewith.

The Lord Mayor having agreeably to an ancient Custom invited the 16 members of the Company (the usual number attending of that occasion) to Breakfast at the Mansion House on the 8th. of November previous to his being sworn into office at Guildhall, and afterwards to return to the Mansion House to Dinner with His Lordship, We procured carriages for the several Members and Clerk (except such as accompanied Mr Treacher and Mr Cordell in their Carriages) who proceeded from Guildhall to the Mansion House at 12 o'Clock, in their Livery Gowns and there breakfasted with the Lord Mayor and Lord Mayor Elect. The members of the Company, as attendant on the Lord Mayor Elect, agreeably to ancient practice took their seats on the left side of the Table in Seniority, the other side being occupied by the Company of Merchant Taylors of which the Lord Mayor is a Member, the Clerk of each Company, sitting at the bottom of the Table.

Immediately after breakfast the Company preceded the Lord Mayor and Lord Mayor Elect to Guildhall, and received them there, being stationed on the left side of the avenue formed for that purpose (the Company of Merchant Taylors occupying the other side) and afterwards proceeded to the Hustings. Still occupying the Station to the left of the Mayor, where the several Oaths were administered to the Mayor, and the various ceremonies attendant thereon took place, after which the late Lord Mayor, Aldermen, Sheriffs, City Officers, and the Members of the Company severally proceeded to offer their congratulations to His Lordship.

We further beg to report that the Company afterwards returned in their Carriages to the Mansion House where they were entertained by His Lordship in the most Splendid and Hospitable manner, and received every mark of respect and attention in His power to bestow, The Company on this occasion (His Lordship having been sworn into Office) occupied the right hand Table in seniority, the Clerk sitting at the bottom.

On the 9th. of November (Lord Mayors Day) the 16 Members of the Company met agreeably to their Summons, at the Albion Aldersgate Street to Breakfast at 10 o'Clock when the final arrangements for the procession of the Company were made as follows

City Marshal on Horseback
Beadle of the Company, with the Staff in
Sash & Favors
Two Porters
and Standard Bearers in dresses with Favors
bearing the
Royal Standard
City Banner   Company's Banner
Lord Mayor's Banner

late Mr Aldn Peckham's Banner
Two Porters
Band of Music
(consisting of 9 Musicians with Favors)
Clerk in his Carriage
Master, Wardens, and Members of the Company
in their Carriages
(Juniors First, Horses Drest)

In this order the Company proceeded to Guildhall and being there joined by the general procession, attended his Lordship to Blackfriars Bridge, and immediately on his going on board the State Barge proceeded in their Carriages to Westminster, (We having been unable to procure a suitable Barge to accompany His Lordship by Water) to receive him on his landing there & to conduct him to the Court of Exchequer in Westminster Hall, and after the usual oaths were taken by His Lordship. and charge delivered by the Chief Baron of the Exchequer, attended him to his Barge on his return to Blackfriars Bridge, and there rejoined the procession and returned to Guildhall.

We have great pleasure in stating that the Lord Mayor has presented to the Company a Crimson Silk Banner, with his Arms, and the emblems of Mayoralty emblazoned thereon,

We further beg to report that in carrying into effect, the arrangements referred to us, the following Expences have been incurred in respect thereof, and the Bills for the same having been severally examined, We have directed them to be paid by the Clerk
Vizt

	£	s	d
To A. Savage for Hire of Carriages – – –	12	0	0
To Chas Stokes, Expences of Band – – –	7	4	0
To Messrs. Searle & Godfrey for providing porters, Standard Bearers and Boat to carry colours –	5	6	6
To Geo Blundell, for Sash for Beadle and favors for procession – – – – – – –	8	19	0
To City Marshal, usual Fee – – – –	2	2	0
To Mesrs. Kay's, Breakfast 9 Nov. – – –	4	18	0
Compliments to Servants at the Mansion House, Coachmen, Footmen, &c. Altering Colours and sundry Expenses – – – – – –	7	10	1
	£47	19	7

All which we submit the Honble Court and remain Gentlemen
Your obedient & faithful Servants

(Signed)   J Hurcombe   Master
                Wm Ruston ⎱
                J P Peacock ⎰ Wardens

In 1822 George Bridges presented the Company with a silver loving-cup, and the Court thanked him for the 'handsome and valuable silver vase, a splendid and lovely memorial of the high and important honours conferred on him by his fellow Citizens'. The Clerk was instructed to place the cup in the safe at Guildhall. (For a full description of the Company's Plate see Appendix IV.)

During the first half of the nineteenth century the Company had some trouble with its Beadles. Barrington Wood, who had been Master of the Company in 1772 and was appointed Beadle in 1781 at £11 per annum, died in 1808. His son, Barrington Wood, was unanimously elected in his place at a salary of £20 a year. But it was ordered that 'the allowances be discontinued except that for quarterage collected at 3s in the pound' for which the new Beadle had to give a security for £100.

In 1814 the Beadle made one of the regular drives to collect arrears of quarterage and collected money from seven members, but there were still another ten in arrears. The Beadle was allowed a new suit of clothes and a hat for his pains. But five years later the Court decided that Barrington Wood was unfit to discharge his duties. Harbin Elderton was elected in his place, with the allowance of a suit of blue clothes and one guinea for a hat. In 1821 the Beadle was given five guineas for his assiduity in collecting quarterage during the preceding year, but in 1824 Harbin Elderton was dismissed and James Davis was appointed Beadle. (In January 1840 Harbin Elderton applied to the Court for relief and was granted £1 a quarter for the rest of the year. In July of that year his widow was paid £3 for expenses in relation to her husband's decease.)

In 1826 the Court appointed a committe to review the Charter and Bylaws, and suggest any alterations thought to be necessary, but the committee reported that no alteration was necessary for the good government of the Company. Two years later the Court passed a resolution, which is still printed in every list of the Livery:

3rd April, 1828

That in future no person shall be chosen or admitted into the offce of Master, Warden or Assistant of the Company who has been a bankrupt, or failed and not paid 20s. in the £. That this Resolution be attached to the printed Lists of the Livery of the Company and that in future all elections that shall not be conformable thereto shall be null and void.

Two years later there was an unusual protest to the Court. Thomas Willis Cooper, son of William Cooper, carpenter, of Hadleigh, Suffolk, was elected to the Court of Assistants. John Parker protested that Cooper had only been admitted to the Livery in 1827 and that he had been elected Assistant over the heads of 150 senior Liverymen. The Court called in Mr Parker and pointed out to him that they had acted in strict conformity with the Charter. As a result of this, a motion was made in the Court in 1831 that 'in future elections there is to be a preference to those who have been longest on the List of Livery, provided that their character and circumstances are considered by the Court in all other respects as a sufficient recommendation.' But when put to the vote, it was 'carried in the negative'.

When in 1833 the Clerk presented to the Court the requisition of the Commissioners appointed to inquire into the existing state of the Municipal Corporations of England and Wales, the Company stood on its dignity. The Clerk was instructed to furnish the information required on the understanding that it was a voluntary matter and to point out that the provision of information was not an admission of the legality of the said Commissioners. The Clerk gave the Commissioners the information in full 'upon the conditional understanding, however, that the same was to be considered as furnished, without prejudice to any of the rights or privileges now enjoyed or exercised by the Company, and that the same should not be brought into a precedent on any future occasion'.

For the first time in many years, and for the last time in the history of the Company, a Freewoman was admitted: in January 1838: 'Jeanette Stoffel, daughter of William Stoffel, Citizen and Wheelwright, was made Free by patrimony and paid 13s 4d'. Her fine was a humble contribution to the funds of the Company, which had long been shrinking and were further affected by the Reform Bill of 1832.

6

Finances, Duties and Privileges

THE DELICATE balance between income and expenditure continued to be a source of anxiety and debate. In 1830 the Court decided that there should be 'no Livery Dinner on Lord Mayor's Day, in consequence of the visit of His Majesty (William IV) to the Corporation of London and because of the state of the funds'. In 1831 a statement on the past four years' finances showed that income had declined from £516 17s 1d in 1827 to £340 os 10d in 1830, but expenditure over the same period had only varied by £482 to £480. It was therefore resolved that 'invitations to visitors at the Lady Day and Michaelmas Courts be in future discontinued and that champagne or other French wine be not introduced'.

When Queen Victoria came to the throne in 1837, the Company was asked what portion of St Paul's Churchyard it would require to erect booths or standings for her Majesty's procession to the Guildhall on 9 November. The Clerk told the Court that after the boys of Christ's Hospital, the Goldsmiths, Fishmongers, and Merchant Taylors had appropriated their spaces, only 115 feet were left for other Companies, and that the expense of fitting up a 30-foot frontage would be between £140 and £150. It was resolved that the state of the funds did not justify such an expense.

In July 1838 the Company was pleased to lend its plate to a Coronation feast given by the City, but a committee appointed to determine the Company's ability to give a Livery dinner delivered a gloomy report:

Gentlemen

We whose names are hereunto subscribed of Your Committee Court to whom it was referred on the 11th. January last to consider of the practicability of providing a Dinner for the Livery of the Company on Lord Mayor's Day, Do report that we proceeded to the consideration of the subject referred to us, and directed the Clerk to lay before us a detailed Statement of the probable Receipts and Expenditure of the Company, calculated chiefly upon the average of the last 3 years . . . by which it appears that there is . . . a deficit of £11.2.4 per annum; which Statement we have hereto annexed for the information of the Company.

It further appears that the present number of the Livery is (including the Master, Wardens & Court of Assistants,) 175 of which about 134 are eligible to be invited under the order of the Court of the 16th January 1794, in relation to the payment of Quarterage—

On reference to the Accounts of the Company for former Years, it appears that the amount of Fines received on the admission of persons to the Livery of the Company, was more than sufficient, to meet the expence of the Dinners annually provided for the Livery, & was in fact considered as the means for providing the same, but we regret to state, that from the period of the passing of the Act to amend the representation of the people in England and Wales (in 1832) by which the Elective Franchise for London, was extended to all Householders of £10 pr. ann. Value, and restricted to such freemen, or such persons as should be entitled to their freedom by birth or servitude, the inducement to Obtain the Elective Franchise, by the Freedom & Livery, either by purchase or in any other mode, has been so much diminished that only one application for the Livery has been made since that period. The Company have therefore been deprived of that portion of their income, formerly derived from such source.

Your Committee therefore, after mature consideration of the subject referred to them, & with an anxious desire for the accomplishment of so desirable an object, are compelled to state to this Honorable Court, that from the present state of the Funds of the Company, arising from the circumstances before referred to and in respect of which, we see no material or immediate prospect of improvement, we are unable to point out any means by which that object can be effected.

That with the view of bringing the ordinary Expenditure of the Company within the amount of its income, we are of opinion that every practicable economy should be exercised, we therefore recommend that the annual payment of £2.2 for providing Gowns on the meetings of the Court, & which are now so seldom required on applications for the Livery, should be discontinued, and that the allowances hitherto payable to the Clerk of £2.10. for making out the annual Charge for quarterage, and one shilling in

Diagrams illustrating dishing

(*Above*) James Benjamin Scott, Clerk
1870–1908 and author of *A Short Account
of the Worshipful Company of Wheelwrights*,
1884; (*right*) Frank W. Robson, Master
in 1923 and first Instructor to a class for
Wheelwrights established in conjunction
with the Carpenters' Company in 1894

the pound on the amount of Quarterage received, be also discontinued, as the amount of Quarterage now received by him
does not bear the same proportion to the whole amount received
as formerly.

All which we submit to the Judgment of Your Worshipful Court;
the 4th July, 1838

(Signed)

Edwd. Conder	Jas. Browning
David Cameron	Robert Day
Edward Jones	W. Beetham
Wm. Beer	Jos. Fleming

Edward Conder was Master of the Company and all the
others were Past Masters, except David Cameron who succeeded Conder in 1839, and Edward Jones who became
Master in 1840. They added:

Statement referred to in the foregoing report—

RECEIPT	£	s	d
Interest on £4,400 Old South Sea Annuities –	132	0	0
Net amount of Quarterage (average of 3 yrs) –	52	16	6
do. of Fees of Admn. of Freeman & Binding apprentices (av) – – – – – – –	12	0	8
Average (17 Yrs) of assistant fines – – –	15	17	3
do. of Fines for Non attendance – – – –	1	9	6
Interest on Stock applicable to the use of the Poor –	7	15	2
	221	19	1
Deficit – – –	11	2	4
	£233	1	5

EXPENDITURE	£	s	d	£	s	d
Av Expence of January Court Dinner –	18	18	6			
April – – – –	17	14	0			
July – – – –	17	19	6			
Oct – – – –	20	9	3			
Mr Jones Vocalist –	4	4	0			
				79	5	3
Allowance towards Expences of Masters (Dinner £30 & £4 4) – – – – – – –				34	4	0
Average Expence of Quarterly poor – – –				18	10	8
do. of Casual poor (amt. of Interest) – –				7	15	2
Salary of Clerk– – – – – – –				31	10	0
Gratuity per order Court – – – – –				21	0	0
Allowance for making out quarterage books – –				2	10	0

F

	£	s	d	£	s	d
Salary to Beadle — — — —	20	0	0			
average of orders of Court — —	5	7	0			
allowance for 40 lists of Livery —	2	2	0			
Common Hall (average) — —		19	6			
Sundries — — — — —		5	0			
				28	13	6
For Sittings at Guildhall per annum — — —				4	4	0
For Livery Gowns — — — — — —				2	2	0
For printing List of Livery entitled to vote under reform act, Stationery, Receipts &c. — —				2	5	10
Payment to the Master, on audit of accounts —				1	1	0
				£233	1	5

Resolved

That this Court agree with the Committee Court in their said report.

The following year, 1839, was also mainly occupied in exploring the possibilities of raising money. It was mournfully agreed that 'no investment in a Government security (and we can admit no other) will increase the funds enough to supply a Dinner.' It was decided that vocalists should be dispensed with at the Quarterly Court Dinner to save the four-guinea fee. At the same time it was decided to prepare a case to enforce the payment of quarterage. In January 1840, after hearing counsel's opinion, the Court ordered that all Liverymen in arrears for two years and upwards be summoned to appear and explain the reasons for their default. In April, four Liverymen paid up and two others pleaded for more time to do so. In July, seven members paid fines amounting in all to £1, and Mr Treacher, who excused himself from becoming an Assistant, was fined £20, later reduced to £10.

In 1841 Benjamin Whinnell Scott, who had succeeded Charles Montague as Clerk to the Company in 1818, resigned, and it seemed to the Court an appropriate time to make an enquiry into the duties and emoluments of the Clerk and the Beadle:

At a Meeting of the Committee Court of the Worshipful Company of Wheelwrights, held at Guildhall on Thursday June 24th, 1841.

The Resolution of the last Court, by which it was refered to the Committee Court 'to enquire into the duties and emoluments of the Office of Clerk to the Company' having been read, the Clerk laid before the Meeting a Statement which had been prepared by direction of the Master, and which was read as follows:

A Statement of the Duties and Emoluments of the Clerk of the Wheelwrights Company, the Emoluments calculated for the last 3 Years.

Duties

To take directions from the Master for summoning the several Courts of the Company, and of the business of the same; To give directions to the Beadle for making out the Summonses for the Court,

To attend the several Courts, Committee Courts and Meetings of the Auditors of the Company and to take minutes of proceedings,

To make fair copy of the said Minutes and of business done out of Court for confirmation at the subsequent Court,

To receive and pay all monies on account of the Company, to keep accounts of the same and to submit a detailed statement thereof annually for examination by the Auditors,

To keep a book of the several Members of the Company and of the quarterage due from each and to bring forward the annual Charge of the same,

To make Statement of Monies received on account of Quarterage from the said book for examination by the Auditors,

To prepare a list annually of such Members of the Company as are entitled to vote for Members of Parliament for the City of London, with their places of residence in conformity with the provisions of the Reform Act and to furnish 3 copies of the same to the Secondaries. To attend the Revising Barristers to certify the same on oath and to answer any questions and afford any information required, in respect of claims & objections relating to the list of the Company,

To admit to the Freedom and Livery Members of the Company, to bind Apprentices, [summons the members in arrear for quarterage: there is a wobbly line partly through and partly under this passage, and it appears to be meant as a deletion] pay the quarterly allowances to the Poor, to account to the Inspector of Stamps for the amount of Duty received on the admission of Freemen, to give directions respecting the several Entertainments of the Company and to check and discharge the several Bills, and to do all such other Acts as may be required in the due discharge of the business of the Company, by direction of the Court of Assistants or the Master and Wardens.

Emoluments

	1838			1839			1840		
	£	s	d	£	s	d	£	s	d
Fees on the admission of Freemen by Servitude and Patrimony – – –	8	16	8	10	16	0	7	1	4
Ditto by Redemption– –	*1	9	0	5	5	0	5	16	0
Ditto in binding Apprentices	6	0	6	1	3	0	2	6	0
Ditto on admission to Livery	—			—			15	0	
Ditto on admission of Assistants – – – –		5	0		2	6		2	6
Salary – – – –	31	10	0	31	10	0	31	10	0
Gratuity, increased from £10.10 to £21, 5th. Oct. 1826 – – – –	21	0	0	21	0	0	21	0	0
	£69	1	2	£69	16	6	£68	10	10

* Note: the fees on Redemption were frequently given to the person introducing the Freeman.

The allowance of £2 10s for making out quarterage books and 1s in the £ on quarterage collected, amounting to about £4 per annum were relinquished on report of Committee 5 July, 1838.

The Committee Court having fully considered the subject, agreed upon the following Report.

To the Master, Wardens and Court of Assistants of the Worshipful Company of Wheelwrights—
Gentlemen,

We whose names are hereunto subscribed of your Committee Court to whome it was refered on the 1st. April last 'to enquire into the duties and Emoluments of the Office of Clerk of the Company', Do report that we have had laid before us a detailed Statement of the Duties of the Clerk and an account of the Emoluments of his Office for the last 3 Years, a copy of which we have caused to be hereunto appended for the information of the Worshipful Court; That your Committee Court proceeded to the consideration of the subject refered to them, and they beg to submit the statement above mentioned to the consideration of the Court, and at the same time to draw the attention of the Court to the Duties and Emoluments of the Office of Beadle. All which we respectfully submit for the consideration of the Worshipful Court.

Guildhall
June 24th. 1841.

(Signed) Geo Wright
Thomas Reece
Wm. Northcott
James Browning
W. Chaffers

George Wright was Master and Messrs Reece and Northcott the Wardens.

When Benjamin Whinnell Scott resigned from the Clerkship, his son, Benjamin Scott, who in January 1841 became a Freeman of the Company by Redemption instead of going to the Glovers to whom he was entitled by patrimony, was a candidate for the office. He was appointed as Clerk temporarily in July and elected in September. His father then presented to the Company a snuff box 'as a small mark of my respect and esteem'. The Court thanked 'their esteemed friend and worthy Clerk . . . for his gentlemanly letter and handsome present of a silver gilt snuff box'.

On 30 September 1841, the Committee Court delivered its report on the Beadle:

> We whose names are hereunto subscribed of your Committee Court to whom it was refered on the 8th. July last, 'to enquire into the Duties and Emoluments of the Office of Beadle of the Company and to report to the next Court their opinion thereon'
>
> Do report, That we directed a Statement of the said Office and the Emoluments thereof, calculated on the average of the last 3 Years; and which Emoluments appear to have amounted to £39.19.6 per ann. £25.7 of which consists of direct payments from the funds of the Company, £10.7 the Allowance of 15 per cent on the Collection of quarterage, the remainder £4.5.6 being composed of Fees on the admission of Freemen & on apprentice bindings etc.
>
> In considering the above allowances it appears to us that the direct payments from the funds of the Company Vizt: £25.7 are greatly disproportioned to the services rendered in respect of the same, inasmuch as the principal duties of the Beadle (beyond the collection of the quarterage and the attendance at Guildhall on Elections to the Livery, for both which duties he receives separate compensation) are, summoning the five usual Courts of the Company attending the same and the dinners which take place on those days.
>
> We therefore recommend, that the Salary in future remain at £20 per annum, but that the alternate annual Gratuities of £3.3 and £7.11 should cease, but in order to afford an additional stimulus to exertion in the collection of the Quarterage, we recommend that the allowance for collecting the same should be increased to 20 per cent or 4/– in the pound. These allowances it is estimated would give the Beadle an annual income in future, including his casual Fees of £35.

We also recommend that the Beadle should be required to live in London or within 7 miles thereof, and that such regulation should take place together with the proposed reductions of the Allowances at Michaelmas 1843, unless the Office should sooner become vacant

We beg to annex for the information of your Worshipful Court, a statement of the duties & Emoluments calculated on the average of the last three years.

All which we have the honor to submit to the judgement of your Worshipful Court; dated this 30th. Sept. 1841.

Geo Wright
Thos Reece
Wm. Northcott
Danl. Weston
Jas. Browning
W. Chaffers

Edward Jones
E. Conder

A Statement of the Duties & Emoluments of the Beadle of the Wheelwrights Company.

Duties

To attend the Clerk from time to time to receive directions in relation to the business of the Company

To receive his directions for summoning all Meetings of the Company and delivering the summonses.

To attend all meetings of the Court, Livery &c.

To attend at Guildhall on all Elections to identify and admit the members of the Livery

To collect the quarterage of the several Members of the Company and keep correct Memoranda of their several places of residence.

To attend the several dinners of the Company.

Emoluments

	£	s	d
Salary – – – – – – – –	20	0	0
Average of Poundage on quarterage for the last 3 years – – – – – – – –	10	7	0
Voted by the Court £3.3 for necessaries and £7.11 for Clothes and Hat—alternate years Average	5	7	0
Fees on admission of Assistants, Livery, Freemen, and binding Apprentices Average of 3 years	1	2	0
For attending Elections & Common Halls – –		13	6
Fees by Court of Assistants, estimated at (say) –	2	10	0
Total average –	£39	19	6

Note: £2 is also paid the Beadle by Order of Court
      towards the Expense of printing Lists of Court
      & Livery and for 20 copies of ditto.

Resolved, That the foregoing report of the Committee Court
be received by this Court.

In spite of these economies, when James Davis 'continued
to be Beadle' in 1842 he was allowed £6 10s for a new suit of
clothes and one guinea for a hat, and the decision on vocalists
at Dinners was rescinded.

Benjamin Scott resigned as Clerk in 1846 on the grounds of
ill-health, and the Court recorded its 'deep sense of his services
. . . its regard for the integrity of his conduct and for the
urbanity of his manners', adding their sincere condolences and
best hopes for a speedy recovery. It appeared later that the real
causes of strain were Benjamin Scott's onerous duties as Chief
Clerk in the Chamberlain's office. He certainly recovered to
become Chamberlain of London in 1858, Master of the Wheelwright's Company in 1864, and did not die until 1892. He was
succeeded as Clerk by his brother, James Renat Scott, who
had become a Freeman of the Company in 1845.

Finances continued to be the main preoccupation of the
Court. In 1849 a committee appointed to enquire into the
state of the funds, reported that the average income for the
past nine years had been £300, whereas the average annual
expenditure had been £315. As quarterage was less every year
and fines were an uncertain source, the Company had to re-
trench. But since payments to the poor were inviolable and
only a small reduction was permissible in the salaries of its
officers, the expenses of the annual Master's Dinner had to be
cut and Quarterly Dinners had to be at the expense of those
who attended.

A special Court was summoned in 1853 to discuss the resolution of the House of Commons to convert Old South Sea
Annuities into a new stock of £110 2½ per cent annuities. The
Company had £4,658 15s 3d in Old South Sea Annuities and
it decided to accept the new stock. But in the following year it
had to sell £150 worth of the new stock for £126 15s to defray

current expenses, and between 1856 and 1858 another £650 worth of stock was sold to keep the Company going. Yet in the latter year it was resolved 'on the occasion of the election by the Liverymen of London of Edward Conder, Master Elect, to be Sheriff of London and Middlesex, That this Court do place the sum of £50 at the disposal of the Master and Wardens for the year ensuing towards the expenses of the Master's Dinner.'

It was, however, a different story in 1859, when yet another committee reported:

> We whose names are hereunto subscribed Your Finance Committee to whom on the 7th. April last it was referred, to examine into & report upon the financial position of the Company
>
> Do certify That in pursuance of such reference we were attended by our Clerk who laid before us a Statement under various heads of the Receipt and Expenditure of the Company for the last 10 years & which is hereunto annexed, & having heard that gentleman at length thereon we after giving the matter our most careful consideration beg to recommend the following for your adoption.
>
> 1stly That £4000 of the New 2.10 per cent stock in the hands of the Company be sold & the proceeds applied in the purchase of £2500 Great Northern Railway 5 per Cent Stock (Preference) in perpetuity & the balance of present Stock amounting to £159.12.9 be sold & retained for the current expenses of the Company.
>
> 2nd. That the allowance heretofore granted by the Court towards the expenses of the Master's Dinner should be reduced from £34.4 to £25 per annum & in connection therewith the Committee strongly recommend that the Masters and Wardens should not in future be required or expected to incur the expense of the entertainment usually known as the Preliminary Dinner
>
> 3rd. That the Livery should in future be invited to dine at the quarterly Court held after the 29th. September instead of in November as heretofore, should this arrangement be sanctioned a saving of equal to £16 per annum will be effected
>
> Your Committee whilst reviewing each head of receipt & expenditure as laid before them by their clerk Mr. Scott are of opinion that the Gratuity of £10.10 heretofore of late years presented to that gentleman should be with held until the Company is in a better Financial position
>
> In concluding Your Committee are of opinion should their report be adopted that a total saving of upwards of £60 will be effected That is to say an increase in the receipts equal to 18 per cent on estimated receipts on the present scale, whilst a reduction

equal to 13 per Cent will be effected as regards to the Expenditure
All of which we submit to the judgement of Your Worshipful
Court

Dated the 7th day of July, 1859.

Signed   Edward Conder

Henry Cameron

Edward Conder Junr.

Joseph Starling

Benjamin Scott.

Resolved and Ordered, That the Report of the Finance Committee be adopted & that it be entered in the minutes.

Benjamin Scott, now Chamberlain, had been admitted to the Court of Assistants in the previous April.

In October the Court decided not to invest the £4,000 in Great Northern Railway, but to buy New India 5 per cent Stock. During the next fifty years there were several changes in the Company's investment policy.

When James Davis resigned as Beadle in 1861 owing to 'increasing age and infirmity coupled with his partial loss of sight', the Court saw a further opportunity for economy. It was proposed to limit the Beadle's duties to attending the Quarterly Courts and to discontinue his allowances. The Beadle would have half-a-guinea for each Court meeting and his allowance of 6s 6d for each day he attended Guildhall for elections of the Livery would be continued. The Clerk was instructed to find a trustworthy person to collect the quarterage, with the customary allowance of 4s in the £, and James Davis was voted £5 a year pension in consideration of 'his long and faithful service'.

While continuing this perpetual financial struggle, the Company was zealous and active in protecting its rights as a Corporate Body and as privileged citizens of the City of London. Early in 1843 they were informed by the Board of Stamps and Taxes that under the Act of 1 & 2 Victoria double Stamp Duty should be paid upon the admission of all Freemen by Patrimony or Servitude. The Court demurred and the Board of Stamps and Taxes consulted the Treasury, after which the Board repeated its demand, but added: 'under the circumstances of the case Their Lordships have authorised the

Board upon these double duties being paid to refund the single duty'.

A Committee Court was set up to consider the matter and, obviously fearing long and costly litigation, it reluctantly gave way. In their reply to the Board the Company said that it 'believed Stamp Duty had been repealed and this was confirmed in the opinion of the late Attorney General and present Solicitor General, but it being a question between the parties entitled and the Government rather than one for the interference of the Court they would be prepared to pay the double duty claimed upon the understanding that the single duty would be returned'. This was followed by a summons to all Freemen who had not paid Stamp Duty to do so immediately.

A much more serious issue cropped up later in 1843. The Common Council had decided to apply to Parliament to alter the conditions of the elective franchise of the City. Among the changes proposed were: that the right of voting for the Lord Mayor, Sheriffs and Corporate Officers, traditionally enjoyed by the Livery at large, should be restricted to those only of the Livery whose names appear on the Parliamentary Revised Register; that Liverymen living more than seven miles from the City would be deprived of their right to vote at municipal elections; that the right of voting should be extended to 'all the occupiers of premises within the wards who are rated to the Consolidated, Sewers and Police Rates'.

The Wheelwrights were the first Company to protest. Their petition was presented by Edward Conder in his place in the Court of Common Council on 14 December 1843:

> To the Right Honourable the Lord Mayor, Aldermen, and Commons of the City of London, in Common Council Assembled, The Petition and Memorial of the Master, Wardens, Assistants and Commonalty of the Art and Mystery of Wheelwrights of the City of London,
> Sheweth, That your Memorialists have read, with regret, a report made to your Honourable Court by a Committee of your Honourable Court, recommending an application to the Legislature for an Act to alter the Act 11 Geo. 1st., chapter 18, intituled 'An Act to regulate Elections in the City of London.'
> That your Memorialists are of the opinion that the alterations

contemplated in the Elective Franchises of the Citizens of London, are calculated to benefit the rich to the prejudice of the poor, by gratuitously conferring on the wealthy merchant and wholesale dealer, those privileges which the more humble retail trader is compelled obtain at a very heavy, and, in many instances inconvenient expense.

That for these and other reasons, your Memorialists are of opinion that the proposed alteration is not only injudicious, but unjust; and ought therefore to be opposed by all legitimate means.

That your Memorialists further consider that such application to the Legislature unnecessary and uncalled for, and rely with confidence on your wisdom to devise some other means, within the powers of your Honourable Court, for extending the Franchise, should it be thought necessary, by reducing the charges of the Freedom of this City, or otherwise, without infringing the ancient Chartered Constitution of the Corporation of London.

The Petition of the Wheelwrights was followed immediately by Petitions and Resolutions against the new measure by the Innholders, Saddlers, Cooks, Cutlers, Playing-card Makers, Clock-makers, Founders, Stationers, Butchers, Goldsmiths, Clothworkers, Pattenmakers, Coopers, Painter Stainers, Mercers and Coach and Coach Harness Makers. After all the petitions had been read and ordered to be printed in the Minutes of the Common Council, a motion was made: 'That Petitions in favour of the Bill for amending the Act of 11 Geo. I., c. 18, for regulating Elections within this City, be now read? Resolved in the affirmative. And such petitions being called for, it did not appear that there were any.'

The outcry against extending the franchise to non-Freemen and depriving many Liverymen of their rights to vote was so great that the Common Council made no further move until February 1845, when it again ordered a committee to prepare another Bill. By April 1852, the London Corporation Bill had obtained a Second Reading in the House of Commons. The Court of the Wheelwrights learned of this 'with surprise, and cannot but dissent from and express disapprobation of a measure, which goes far to deprive the Freemen & Livery of their ancient Company of those privileges they have obtained either by Inheritance, Servitude or purchase.'

Opposition was still strong and further petitions of the Livery

Companies were referred to the Standing Order Committee of the House of Commons. Benjamin Scott was one of the City officers examined in support of the Bill. After the Corporation's case was closed, Sir Walter Riddell stated the case of the Companies who were petitioners against the Bill. He spoke for about two hours, but called no witnesses. The committee then deliberated in private for two hours and a half, after which the parties were called in and informed that the 'Preamble of the Bill was not proved'. Discussions and amendments dragged on for another six years and in 1859 a similar Bill was introduced, to be finally withdrawn in July 1860. When the Mercers wrote to the Wheelwrights in 1854 about the expenses incurred in opposing the Corporation Bill, the Wheelwrights replied by sending a copy of their Resolution of April 1852. They clearly felt that they had fulfilled their obligation.

7

Interlude for Melodrama

THE YEAR 1855 opened with a shock.

> 11th. January, 1855. The Court hears with feelings of the deepest horror and regret the dreadful occurrence which has taken place since their last meeting in the assassination of their late Upper Warden Mr. Geo Moore, and while lamenting most sincerely the loss they have sustained as a Court by his decease, desire to record their Sympathy with his family in the distressing event which has so suddenly deprived them of his Counsels as a Father & a Friend.
>
> Ordered, that a copy of the above resolution be forwarded to Mr. William Moore, the brother of the deceased.

The reason for the murder of George Moore, elected Upper Warden in the previous October, remained a mystery and the trial of the murderer became a *cause célèbre*. *The Times* reported on 9 December 1854:

> A twofold murder of the most atrocious and determined character took place last night, about a quarter before 9 o'clock, in Warren-street, Fitzroy-square.
>
> The victims are, first, Mr. George Moore, soda-water manufacturer, of No. 73, Warren-street; and secondly Mr. Charles Collard, greengrocer, of No. 74, in the same street, who, upon hearing the cry of 'murder' in the adjoining house, ran out, and in an attempt to arrest the assassin, was shot through the body.
>
> The circumstances under which this most diabolical tragedy took place are as follows:—About a-quarter past 8 o'clock last night an engineer named Barthelemy, who has been occasionally employed by Mr. Moore in his business as a soda-water manufacturer, called upon him in Warren-street. He was accompanied by a young woman, and both were received by Mr. Moore as friends, and conducted into the back parlour, where according to the statement of Mr. Moore's female servant, they remained together for

93

about 20 minutes without anything having occurred to excite her observation.

At the expiration of that time her attention was arrested by the sound of something like a scuffle. She listened for a moment, when the noise increased and a cry of 'Murder' followed. She ascended the kitchen stairs, and as she came in view of the back parlour door, she saw her master and the engineer come out and engage in what appeared to her to be a deadly struggle in the passage. Before she could recover herself, she heard a pistol go off, and the next moment her master fell a corpse.

Barthelemy instantly left the house by the front door, but being met by the unfortunate man Collard, who opposed his escape, the assassin returned into the house, shutting the door after him, and instantly retreated by the garden entrance, which opens into the New-road. Poor Collard, on finding his intention of arresting the murderer in Warren-street defeated, immediately hastened round into the New-road, anticipating that the assassin might endeavour to escape by that route. He was right, but his judgement and admirable presence of mind have cost him his life, and left a family of young children fatherless with a widowed mother. Barthelemy was in the act of scaling the garden wall and jumping on to the pavement in the New-road, when Collard seized him.

The murderer instantly drew a pistol from his pocket and shot the courageous fellow in the abdomen. The ball took fell effect and Collard fell helpless on the ground, the assassin rushing off, and, for a moment seeming to escape. But, providentially this second murder had been witnessed by another person, who followed the wretch and speedily made him prisoner. . . .

Mr. Superintendent Foxall with Inspector Checkley were soon upon the spot investigating the matter, and from what they discovered no doubt seems to exist that the murder of Mr. Moore was one of the most cold-blooded and determined crimes ever perpetrated. The back parlour of the murdered man's house presents all the appearance of a most deadly struggle having taken place. The walls are spotted with blood in several places, and the furniture, including a strong and substantial mahogany chair, broken to pieces. Upon the floor of the room was found a piece of broken cane, heavily loaded at one end with lead. There are marks on the deceased's person which show that he must have been struck with this weapon in the first instance, and the handle to the bludgeon has been broken into two pieces.

Mr. Moore, after having been brutally ill-treated by his assailant, seems to have almost succeeded in overpowering him, upon which the assassin drew from his pocket the pistol and shot his victim in the face.

There are marks in the room which lead to the supposition that, at the moment of the first attack taking place, the deceased was in the act of opening a soda-water bottle. . . .

When the prisoner was examined at Marlborough-street police station, he was recognised as Emmanuel Barthelemy, a 32-year-old Frenchman who, in 1853 had fought another Frenchman, Frederick Cournet, in a duel at Egham. Cournet's pistol was jammed with a rag and he was killed, but Barthelemy was sentenced to only two months for manslaughter. Policemen who searched Barthelemy after his arrest found that he had a ticket for the Hamburg boat, sailing the next morning, a pair of pistols, twenty-four ball cartridges, some percussion caps, a nine-inch dagger, two door keys, 8½d in money and three cigars. The mysterious veiled woman who accompanied Barthelemy to George Moore's house was never found, and Barthelemy himself, 'a remarkably fine-looking young man, about middle stature and with a foreign expression of countenance', maintained a 'rigid silence' throughout the police-court proceedings and the trial. This took place at the Central Criminal Court on 4 January 1855 before the Lord Chief Justice Campbell and Mr Justice Crowder. He was indicted for the murder of Charles Collard and 'the prisoner, who had elected to be tried by a jury composed half of foreigners, challenged several of the foreign jurymen'.

The most interesting pieces of evidence at the trial were the statements of Charlotte Bennett, Mr Moore's servant, who said:

> The prisoner had been employed by my master to repair the engine for manufacturing ginger beer and soda water. I had never heard him converse with my master. He had been at the house more than twice, probably about half-a-dozen times; but my master was never with him except on the night in question.
>
> William Smith, a police constable, said: There was an iron safe in the front room of Mr. Moore's house, and I picked up the key of that safe upon the floor in the back parlour. There was a door by which the two rooms communicated.
>
> Charlotte Bennett, the servant, was recalled, and she said that Mr. Moore kept his books and cashbox in the safe in question, and always had the key in his pocket. She also said that she had never seen such an instrument (the bludgeon) as the one that had been produced, in the house before the night in question.

Mr Collyer, QC, defending the prisoner, offered the ingenious argument that Barthelemy should have been indicted for killing Mr Moore, in which case he would only have been guilty of manslaughter, and suggested that in the case of Collard the pistol went off accidentally. The jury took three-quarters of an hour to bring in a verdict of guilty, coupled with a strong recommendation to mercy, but the Lord Chief Justice, in his address to the prisoner, commented: 'I don't know upon what ground the recommendation is given. I look upon your crime as one of great atrocity and without any mitigation; I will, however, lay that recommendation before the advisers of the Crown, but I exhort you to prepare to undergo the dreadful sentence which I am about to pass.'

The death sentence produced a spate of letters and protests to the newspapers, mainly from Frenchmen, who claimed that since the death penalty had been abolished in France, Barthelemy should not hang; others claimed the recommendation for mercy was inconceivable.

On 11 January 1855 *The Times*, quoting an evening paper, published an account of Barthelemy in which it said that the Frenchman had been imprisoned for causing a political disturbance in Paris and on his release shot the gendarme who had denounced him. He was given a long sentence, but released after the fall of Louis Philippe and took a prominent part in the great insurrection of 1848. It was suggested that the death of Cournet was engineered by the French police and that the

French republican exiles, who as a body are most respectable gentlemen, avoided him as a police agent. . . . Why Collard was murdered by Barthelemy is obvious; not so, however, the murder of Moore. It is perhaps one of those things that will remain for ever in obscurity; but so far as the facts go, every circumstance in connexion with it points to predetermination, while the key of the safe found on the floor tells of meditated robbery as well. The probability is that, having worked for Moore, he was well aware that Moore made his weekly payments on a Saturday morning; and the wages of Moore's men were known by him therefore to be in the safe in the back parlour on the Friday night, the night of the murder. The supposition explains the ticket for Hamburg (the Hamburg boat sails on the Saturday morning), the heavy bludgeon, the poniard, and the loaded pistols.

The Court in Session, 1 October 1969: (*from left to right*) D. F. Smeed, the Beadle; E. W. Bales, Assistant; F. C. Schilling, Assistant; D. T. Russell, Assistant; S. W. Howard, Assistant; R. E. Bates, Assistant; D. G. Humphreys, Assistant; F. G. Wills, Assistant; Col E. G. Bates, Past Master; M. H. Hinton, the Clerk; Dr G. S. Udall, the Upper Warden; R. E. Stubington, the Master; H. S. Dodson, the Renter Warden; Col H. Brookhouse, Past Master; A. W. White, Past Master; Alderman H. Murray Fox, Past Master; M. J. W. Russell, Past Master; J. B. Hepworth, Assistant; T. J. Metcalf, Assistant; W. F. Newbury, Assistant

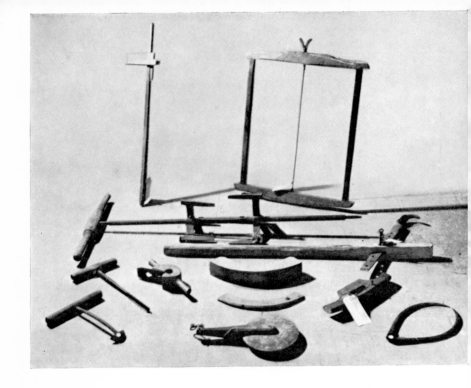

車大工組合　(The Worshipful Company of Wheelwrights)

　　ロンドン市の他の大部分の組合と違って，車大工組合は宗教団体として出発したので
はなく，輸送手段としての馬車の必要性が17世紀になって増大したのにつれて注目され
るにいたった団体である。だから組合員はことごとく職人であった。彼らは1631年に組
合結成を図ったが実現せず，1670年にチャールズ2世が，彼らに車大工業を掌握させる
勅許を与えるにいたり，やっと組合設立に成功した。こんにちでは他の多くの組合と同
様，慈善事業に尽力している。

車大工の道具
BB 1　のこぎり(bettye saw)——木材を大輪用に切る。
BB 2　幅（や）削りなた(spokeshave)
BB 3　幅（や）削りかんな(jarvis)
BB 4　きり（スプーン形）——穴あけ用
BB 5　きり（スペード形）——穴あけ用
BB 6　型板(temple)——大輪の型取り用。
BB 7　大輪(felloe)
BB 8　外側カリパス(outside callipers)——測径両脚器。
BB 9　すべり環(traveller)——車輪の円周をはかるための回転円板。
BB10　幅（や）はめ器(spoke set gauge)
BB11　幅（や）レバー(spoke dog)
BB12　車軸（じく）はめ機(boxing engine)——車軸（じく）を受けるベアリング
　　　　(box)を，こしきの中心にはめこむ機械。

Photograph with Japanese text of some of the Company's tools at the exhibition
in Tokyo of 'Treasures and Traditions of the City of London', September—October
1969

In a long description of Barthelemy's execution in front of
Newgate Gaol on 22 January before a crowd which, 'not-
withstanding the inclemency of the weather, was very great',
The Times reported:

> The only allusion he has made to the 'affair', as he has always
> termed this double murder, was one day in the presence of Mr.
> Davis (the prison chaplain), when he gave the only explanation
> of the circumstances under which the life of Mr. Moore was taken.
> This explanation was to the effect that the woman by whom he was
> accompanied at the time in question was an illegitimate child, and
> she was in the habit of receiving money through Mr. Moore. At
> the period of the murder some money was owing to her, and he
> accompanied her to the house for the purpose of obtaining it, and
> he declared that he had no idea at the time of committing any act
> of violence. He says, however, that upon Mr. Moore refusing to
> pay the money that was due a quarrel took place, and this led to
> the fatal result. With regard to the deadly instrument, the cane
> stick with the heavy leaden knob, the handle of which was found
> tied round his wrist when he was taken into custody, he asserted
> most positively that he did not take it with him to Mr. Moore's
> house, but that it was lying on the table, and he admits that he took
> it up and struck the unfortunate deceased, and that he also broke
> the chair with the same instrument.

So whether the unfortunate Upper Warden was being black-
mailed or was the victim of attempted robbery with violence
will never be known.

8

Expansion and Education

THE WHEELWRIGHTS Company continued to have internal difficulties. In October 1856 William Gould, an Assistant, wrote an angry letter after the election of James Browning as Master for the second time—he had previously served in 1831—in which Gould made it plain to the Clerk, that he thought he had been snubbed and passed over. Complaining of the 'uncourteous treatment' he pointed out that he did not ask to be placed on the Court, but rather expressed reluctance to it. He contended that either his election as Master should have followed in due course or he should have been consulted as to the rightness of its postponement. Gould concluded: 'I have arrived at the conclusion that I am in the way of all past Masters serving the office a second time, which it would appear they have an ambition to do. As however I do not choose to look on until they are of opinion that I may have obtained a position enabling me to fill the Office of Master respectably, I now unalterably resign all connection with the Wheelwrights Company.'

Soon there came the first signs of growing affluence and expansion. In 1864 it was resolved that the Court *and its ladies* dine together on Wednesday 29 June, and in 1865 four new Liverymen were admitted, including Ernest Charles Nolda, whose family came from Munster in Westphalia. The Master, William Brass, was thanked by the Court for his interest in introducing them. Two years later the Clerk was instructed to pay the £3 stamp duty on all admissions to the Freedom and Livery from the funds of the Company.

Even so, there was another financial crisis in 1870, when a Committee reported that the yearly income was not expected to exceed £150. This resulted in a recommendation that the Livery Dinner be held every other year; that the April and July Courts should be purely nominal; that no pensioner of the Company should receive more than £10 a year; that printing costs should be kept down to £10 a year; that the Clerk's salary be not more than £35 a year and that he should receive no additional gratuities.

In October 1870 James Renat Scott resigned after twenty-four years service as Clerk. The Court praised him' for his zeal and faithful service, trusting that he be speedily restored to his accustomed health.' He was admitted to the Court and became Master of the Company in 1875. James Benjamin Scott was elected Clerk at a salary of £31 10s. At the same time Thomas Offill, who had succeeded Thomas Higgs as Beadle in 1868, also resigned, and Mr H. Hammond was elected in his place.

The Summer Dinner was revived as an annual event in 1873 and in the same year a sum not exceeding ten guineas was voted towards emblazoning the Company's arms in one of the windows of the new Library at Guildhall. At the same time the Court resolved to provide a badge to be worn by the Master, at a cost of not more than fifty guineas. The first design submitted was not approved and in October 1873 a second badge was placed on the table and a copy of the design was sent to each Member of the Court 'at a cost of not more than 12s 6d'. This was approved and the badge was first worn by the Master at the Livery Dinner in October 1873.

Two Members of Parliament, Sir Edward William Watkin and Mr James Fortescue Harrison were invited to the Master's Dinner in 1876, and eighteen months later they were both elected to the Court of Assistants. In 1880 the Court expressed its 'best thanks to Sir E. Watkin, Bart, MP, Senior Warden, for placing a special train at the disposal of the Company on the occasion of its summer entertainment on July 1'. Sir Edward William

Watkin was in a unique position to provide a special train, for he was one of the great railway promoters of the nineteenth century. At that time he was Chairman of the Manchester, Sheffield & Lincolnshire Railway (which he later converted into the Great Central by building a new line from Sheffield to Marylebone); Chairman of the South Eastern Railway; and Chairman of the Metropolitan Companies. He had been a Director of both the Great Eastern and Great Western Railways; he had built a new line from Manchester to Liverpool, and was responsible for the through route from Cardiff to Liverpool. He helped to build the Athens to Piraeus railway and in 1872 formed a Channel Tunnel Company and began excavations between Folkestone and Dover. When the Board of Trade obtained an injunction to stop him, on the grounds that he was infringing the Crown's foreshore rights, he used the compnay for boring for, and finding coal in the neighbourhood of Dover. Watkin was Member of Parliament for Stockport from from 1864 to 1868 and for Hythe from 1874 to 1895. He was knighted in 1868 and created a baronet in 1880.

Watkin was an enthusiastic Wheelwright and sat on many of the Company's committees. After he had served as Master in 1881, the Court thanked him for the manner in which he had discharged his office and 'for his courtesy and general behaviour to his brethren of the Court and especially for his generous consideration of the Livery'. (He was succeeded as Master by James Fortescue Harrison, who had been MP for Kilmarnock Burghs from 1874 to 1880.) When in 1882 the Wheelwrights were asked to appoint a representative on the Livery Committee set up by Common Hall to take measures 'for the defence of the Rights and Privileges of the Livery', Sir Edward Watkin was chosen.

In 1880 another bothersome Royal Commission was set up to enquire into the City of London Livery Companies, and once again the Wheelwrights stood on their dignity. They did not reply to the massive questionnaire sent out by the Commission and in January 1881 the Clerk made a general application to the several Livery Companies:

32 Coal Exchange,

14th January, 1881.

The Clerk to the Worshipful Company of—

Dear Sir,

The Court of the Worshipful Company of Wheelwrights have appointed a Committee to consider the enquiries issued by the City of London Livery Companies' Commission and in reference to such enquiries they have directed their Master (Sir E. Watkin, Bt., M.P.) their Wardens (J. F. Harrison Esq. and E. R. Cook Esq.) & Benjn. Scott Esq. Chamberlain of London, one of the Court of Assistants, to make enquiry of the several Livery Companies on the following point—Whether they have respectively obtained any opinion of Counsel, as to the legal & constitutional competence of the said Commission to make the enquiries which it has issued.

The above named Gentlemen will be much obliged if you will give them (through me) an answer to the above, and in the event of any such opinion having been taken by the Worshipful Company of— they will esteem it a particular favour if your Court will authorize your giving them a copy of the same.

I am Dear Sir,

Yours faithfully,

J. B. Scott

Clerk to the Wheelwrights Co.

In March, the Clerk reported that out of the seventy-four applications sent out, he had received forty-nine answers. None of those replying had taken counsel's opinion, though nine might do so. He also reported that the Joiners' Company had already sent in its reply but the Wax Chandlers did not intend to reply unless obliged. The Clothworkers replied as follows:

Clothworkers Hall
Mincing Lane, E.C.
17 Jany, 1881

Dear Sir,

Replying to your letter of the 14th. inst I have to inform you that this Court has not thought it necessary to obtain any opinion of Counsel as to the legal & constitutional competence of the London Livery Companies Commission to make the enquiries which it has issued. There is no doubt that a Royal Commission has no power to enforce the rendering of information *in invitos* unless armed with special Statutory Powers—In the case of the Public Schools Enquiry and the University Commission it was so likewise. I send you a letter embodying the views of this Company

and the Returns are in a forward state of preparation & will be submitted to this Court in the course of the Spring.

I am Sir,

Yours faithfully,

Owen Roberts

Clerk to the Compy.

The enclosure stated that the Clothworkers would give
practically a full disclosure of their affairs,

> subject to some Reservations and to strong protest against their
> action being construed as an admission derogating from the
> Rights, Privileges & Franchises vested in the Freemen and Livery-
> men of the Company. . . . It is however considered highly desirable
> that those Companies adopting in principle the propriety or ex-
> pediency of replying to the Commissioners' Interrogatories should
> direct a conference between their Executive Officers before finally
> determining on certain points which arise in connection with the
> questions, so that the course adopted in reference thereto, may be
> so far as possible uniform & consistent.

The Wheelwrights were still not satisfied. Their minutes
record: 'A letter was then read from Mr H. D. Warr, Secretary
to the City of London Liveries Commission requesting that the
returns might be furnished by the end of April. Resolved: That
the Clerk do acknowledge the same'.

The Court then considered counsels' opinion which had been
obtained by the Livery Companies Association from J. W. Chitty,
QC, MP, Horace Davey, QC, MP, and R. S. Wright. This was
to advise that the Commission had no power to enforce the
discovery of trust property, but thought it likely that the Company would think it reasonable to do so; adding that details
of other property could be reasonably denied and a formal
statement should be inserted to make this clear. The Company
then answered the Commission's questions, with the protest
that 'this information is afforded voluntarily, as was that which
was rendered to the Commission which sat in 1837'. The
Secretary to the Commission wrote back, thanking the Company for its 'highly complete and well arranged returns', but
if the Commission was satisfied, the Junior Warden was not.
In February 1881 Mr Edward Rider Cook wrote a short sharp
letter to the Clerk: 'I am so dissatisfied with the proceedings of

the "Wheelwrights" that I have made up my mind to resign my position of Warden and I suppose as a consequence that of Member of the Court.' The Clerk later reported that he had found Mr Cook still determined to resign, so the resignation was accepted.

Still the correspondence with the Royal Commission dragged on. In 1882 the Commissioners asked the Court whether it would like to send a representative to give oral evidence. The Court did not like, 'considering the exhaustive replies already sent', and added that if any additional explanations are required, let them ask for the same in writing. In 1883 the Court again resolved 'that it is inexpedient either to send a representative or in any way appear before the Commission'. When, after years of deliberation, the Royal Commission recommended introducing a Parliamentary Bill to reform the Livery Companies and divert large parts of their funds to public utilities in the Metropolis, the Wheelwrights wrote to the Twelve Great Companies asking them to stand firm against any such proposals, and they were assured that those Companies would do so.

Although financial problems continued to occupy the attention of the Court during the last quarter of the nineteenth century, it is clear that the generosity of the increasing number of wealthy men who became Liverymen, Assistants, Wardens and Masters was enlarging both the prosperity and the prestige of the Wheelwrights. An instance is their treatment of the Clerk, James Benjamin Scott, who had been appointed in 1870 at a salary of £31 10s. In 1875 the Company granted him a gratuity of ten guineas and increased his annual salary to £42 and in 1897 'the Court were pleased to increase his yearly honorarium to £52 10s'.

In January 1884 the Clerk was requested to prepare a short history of the Company to be issued annually with the Lists of the Livery at a sum not exceeding £15. James Scott acted with some expedition, for in May 1884 the Court ordered that '250 copies of *The History of the Company* be printed on large paper with additions by way of appendices and 100 of them neatly bound for members of the Court and others'.

In 1887 another 1,000 copies of *The History* were printed, and in the following years it was 'Resolved that our worthy and esteemed Clerk, Mr J. B. Scott, having taken very considerable trouble in preparing the history of the Company of Wheelwrights a douceur of £25 be given to mark our appreciation of the special ability and services to the Company on this and other occasions'.

It was decided that the Company's gifts to the Quarterly Poor and the Casual Poor should not be charged in any way to the general fund, but that all payments should be made from the Poor's Box. Those eligible for pensions were divided into two classes: the first, for Liverymen and their widows only, for whom there would be three pensions at £10 per annum; the second, for which daughters of Liverymen could be eligible, four pensions at £5 per annum. To meet these expenses every Freeman and Liveryman would be expected to pay 10s on admission. This rule came into force in 1881 and in the following year, after another long financial report by a special committee, it was resolved that the Clerk should present a quarterly financial statement of the Company's affairs at each Court meeting.

Charles Dew Miller, Master in 1885, presented a gold chain for the Master's badge, and the provision of Past Masters' badges was approved in 1886. The first design proved too costly and another was made for seven guineas, with 4s 6d extra allowed for the inscription.

At the January Court in 1887 the Clerk read a letter from Messrs Bishop & Clarke announcing that all the Company's banners had been burnt. Messrs Bishop and Clarke were told to replace them by April, and were asked what compensation they were prepared to pay as the Company considered the banners to be of particular 'value on account of their antiquity'. The Clerk reported to the April Court that the banners had not been replaced and that 'no notice had been taken of our request'. New banners were provided by July, but there is no mention of compensation.

That was the Jubilee Year of Queen Victoria and, to mark the occasion, the Quarterly Poor were given one guinea each from the Poor's Box. But when the Lord Mayor asked for support for the Imperial Institute, the Wheelwrights replied that 'while loyally congratulating Her Most Gracious Majesty on the Jubilee, they felt unable to contribute'. The Wheelwrights were not being mean, for a committee report of 1890 shows that 'outside the Company's ordinary expenditure', they had paid in the past few years:

	£	s	d
Master's Badge – – – – – –	68	0	0
Donation to the Indian Famine Relief Fund –	21	0	0
Window in Guildhall – – – – –	10	10	0
Livery Gowns – – – – – – –	20	0	0
Royal Commission Expenses – – – –	76	0	0
City and Guilds Institute – – – – –	210	0	0
Banner with the Company's Arms – – –	20	0	0
Testimonials – – – – – – –	25	0	0
Donation to the International Health Exhibition –	100	0	0
Badges for Past Masters – – – – –	113	12	6
History of Company – – – – – about	110	0	0

The committee suggested that because of the cost, trouble and irritation caused by the collection of quarterage, it should be compounded at £2, and that the collector's commission should be reduced to 2s 6d in the pound. This was approved by the Court, and the procedure continued until 1908. In 1891 the fine for election on the Court, which had stood at £15 since 1719, was raised to £25, and shortly afterwards to £50.

Apart from finance there were other matters of procedure to be considered. In the minutes for 3 April 1884 the Court meeting is dismissed in two words: 'No quorum'. This difficulty recurred until in 1891 when a special committee was set up to decide what constituted a quorum and how they could ensure the attendance of the requisite number. This committee reported that under the Charter the only provision for a quorum was that 'the greater part of the Court of Assistants' must be present when the election or removal of officers of the

Company was involved. It would therefore be legal to make a new bylaw, defining a quorum for carrying out any other of the Company's business. But the committee also believed that before a new bylaw could be created it would have to be considered not only by the Master, Wardens and Assistants, but also by the commonalty of the Wheelwrights, and this procedure was considered to be too cumbersome. So the committee proposed that the Clerk should nominate thirteen Assistants to attend each meeting of the Court in rota and that it should be obligatory for those nominated to attend. It was also proposed that the original bylaw of 1670 be revived and enforced, by which Assistants were liable to be fined for non-attendance or coming late to a Court meeting. These measures were put into force immediately, but at the April Court in 1891 five of those on the rota failed to attend. The excuses offered by three of them were accepted, the others were fined 2s 6d for non-attendance. Two others were fined 1s each for being late. (In 1913 the quorum for a meeting of the Court was reduced to ten.)

At the same Court the committee produced an analysis of attendances over the five years from 1886 to 1890. Top scorers were John Robbins (Master 1892) with 9 out of a possible 9, William Lemon (Master 1887) and Thomas Baptie (Master 1889) with 22 each out of 24. Bottom of the list were John King Farlow (Master 1872) with 2 out of 24, and Sir Edward Watkin, who had not appeared at all. No doubt he was too busy trying to get his private Bill, authorising his Channel-tunnel project, through Parliament. He introduced it three times without success.

Another committee was appointed in 1897 'to consider the whole question of nominations & election to the Court of Assistants'. It reported:

> We have had examined the Charter, Byelaws & orders of the Court & find there are no restrictions in the Charter & Bye Laws as to the form of nominations & elections—they only provide that 'in the place of any Assistant dying or removing, the Master, Wardens & Assistants for the time being shall elect & choose an able & sufficient person of the said Company'

In the replies to the Commissioners in 1837 Mr. B. W. Scott, the then Clerk stated: 'The election takes place by open vote viz; show of hands or by ballot on the nomination by some member of the Court. More than one candidate is generally proposed on a vacancy. No instance has occurred of one candidate only being proposed & rejected.'

In the rough draft appears the following—ruled through— 'The Court have for many years past invariably elected persons from the Livery of the Company who have expressed their desire become members of the Court of Assistants & although the Court have been desirous to act upon a principle of seniority in such election considerable objections have presented themselves from the age & unwillingness of persons from other circumstances taking on themselves an office at least burthensome in point of expense.'

The following is the reply returned by myself to the Commissioners in 1881: 'Any member of the Livery who has not become a Bankrupt or compounded with his creditors is eligible for membership of the Governing Body. This preference given to the Livery is not prescribed by the Charter of any ByeLaw, but has been the invariable custom since the Grant.'

'When the Charter was granted 3 Feb. 1670 & the ByeLaws framed (12 Oct. 1670 & 3 April 1714) there were no Livery only Freemen. The first Livery was granted 7 Decr. 1773 limiting the number to 100. This number was increased in 1792 to 150 & in 1817 to 250 at which number it remains still.'

'An election to the Court of Assistants takes place upon a vacancy occurring thro' the death, retirement or removal of a member according to the provisions of the Charter. The method adopted to fill up each vacancy is as follows:—The Clerk reports the decease of the member or other circumstance attending such vacancy & the Court appoints a day (usually the next Quarterly Court), at which the election shall take place, due notice whereof to be inserted in the summons. The Court then elect from those in nomination after they have been duly proposed & seconded. The election takes place either by show of hands or ballot. For the last few years it has been conducted by show of hands, very rarely more than one name having been proposed although several may have been in nomination. The last election by ballot was in 1851.'

Since 1881 the ballot has been used more frequently.

The present system of nomination appears therefore to have grown up & there is no express order bearing on the subject.

The following orders regulating nominations have been passed at different times by the Court.

3rd April, 1828

That in future no person shall be chosen or admitted into the office of Master, Warden or Assistant of the Company who hath been a bankrupt or failed or not paid 20/- in the £. That this

resolution be attached to the printed Lists of the Livery of the
Company & in future all elections that shall not be conformable
thereto, shall be null and void.

2nd October, 1879

That no member of the Court shall be entitled to have more
than one Liveryman in nomination for the Court at one time.

6th October, 1892

That no Liveryman shall be eligible for nomination to the
Court of the Company until he has been 3 years on the Livery.

That a Liveryman in nomination for the Court shall not be
eligible for election until 1 year after the date of such nomination.

We then considered the methods adopted by the different Companies which we find vary considerably depending in some cases
on the wording of the Charter & ByeLaws but generally on
custom.

In a few Companies the Liverymen nominally elect, but they are
generally so bound down by regulations & precedents that they
possess no real power.

In some cases the rule of seniority is followed—provided there
is no objection to the candidate.

In others, where Stewards are elected from the Livery, the
Assistants are chosen from those who have served or fined for the
office.

In some of the smaller Companies a system has grown up of
having a list of the Senior Livery—in some cases 12, in some as
many as 24. These remain in nomination unless withdrawn at their
own request & to these are added any specially nominated in
view of the election. The latter are however almost invariably
elected.

The simplest form, which is adopted by several Companies, is
to ask for nominations when a vacancy occurs & elect at the next
Court from such nominations.

We cannot find any Company that nominates precisely in the
same way as the Wheelwrights Co but it must be remembered
that whilst we have divided the Companies into certain well
marked systems they all vary slightly in detail.

We therefore recommend as follows:

That the present list of nominations be expunged.

That in future the Court do ask for nominations on a vacancy
being announced & elect at the next Court those so nominated
after they have been duly proposed and seconded & it be an
instruction to the Clerk to make enquiries in the interim whether
the person so nominated is willing to serve. All nominations are to
terminate with the election.

That the order of the Court 6th. October 1892 'That a Liveryman in nomination for the Court shall not be eligible for election
until 1 year after the date of such nomination' be rescinded.

All of which we submit to the judgment of this Honorable Court—Dated 30th September, 1897.

> (Signed) Chas. C. Paine
> J. J. Runtz
> W. Mann Cross
> J. Ebenezer Saunders.

Resolved, That the foregoing report be adopted and carried into effect.

(Charles Cleverly Paine was Master, Runtz and Cross were Wardens, and Saunders a Past Master who had served in 1874 and 1893.)

In 1900 members of the Court were required to sign a form acknowledging that they ceased to be members if they became insolvent 'or for a period exceeding three years absent myself from all meetings'.

The Company had also again turned its attention to the Trade, after an interval of nearly a century. In 1872 a meeting was held at the Mansion House to consider an exhibition by the Livery Companies of London to promote technical education. James Ebenezer Saunders, JP, who served as Master of the Company in 1874 and again in 1893, represented the Wheelwrights. But apart from another meeting at Drapers Hall, nothing practical was done until 1881, when the Court resolved to contribute £210 to the City & Guilds of London Institute for the advancement of technical education. The money was to be paid over four years at £52 10s a year for prizes in special industries. This contribution gave the Company the right to appoint a representative to the Board of Governors, and Sir E. Watkin was appointed for four years.

In 1892 the Clerk to the London County Council wrote to ask how the Company was assisting in technical education. The Wheelwrights replied that there were no further funds available beyond what they were already spending; but in 1894 came a real advance. In January that year the Court appointed a Technical Education Committee, which reported in April:

> In pursuance of the order of your Worshipful Court that the Committee appointed in January last should consider the prac-

ticability & if advisable establish a class for Wheelwrights in connection with the Carpenters Co for 3 years at a cost not exceeding £50 per annum

I beg to report that your Committee met a Committee of the Carpetners Co at their Training School at 155a Great Titchfield St. where they were shown all the different class-rooms & had explained to them the system & the cost at which the other classes were worked.

The Carpenters Company agreed to provide a suitable room & gas if your Worshipful Company would appoint an Instructor & bear the cost of tools, timber & other incidental expenses. The Carpenters Co. have since agreed to provide the benches required for the students.

Your Committee having decided to proceed in the matter inserted advertisements for an Instructor & drew up a card which they sent to all the Wheelwrights, wagon, cart & van Builders in the London Directory.

Fifteen answers were received in reply to the advertisement from which number the Committee selected 5 who attended.

From these they eventually selected Mr Frank Robson of W. & J. Robson of 60 Farringdon Road who was appointed to give two classes a week during the Term at the rate of £8 per term & half the fees received.

Posters & a syllabus of the classes were then drawn up & sent round to the Trade with a circular asking for their co-operation.

The size of the room allotted your Committee at Titchfield St. compelled them to limit the number of students to 8, but it is gratifying to know that more than double that number have applied showing the want of such a class. The Committee hope soon to make arrangements by which the number of students may be increased.

It was arranged that the classes should commence on 1st. March & be held every Tuesday and Thursday from 6.30 to 9 p.m. up to the 12th April—thus completing a half Term of 6 weeks. The 2nd Term (13 weeks) will commence on April 24th & continue till about the 26th July. There will be 3 terms in the year.

Unfortunately owing to the illness of Mr. Robson, the Instructor, the classes did not commence before March 13th. He has however arranged to give 3 additional classes so that the Term may terminate as arranged on 12th. inst.

The Committee has arranged to hold joint Committees with the Carpenters Co once in each Term to confer on matters arising from time to time.

The Committee have had to purchase Tools, Drawing materials, timber &c. which have cost nearly £30.

This however is a capital Expenditure which should not be required again unless indeed the class was very largely increased.

They have also spent £5.18.3 in advertising, Postage & other Incidental Expenses & have incurred a bill for Stationery. The fees received for the present half Term amount to 13s.

In October 1894 the Master, William Shepherd, the Wardens and members of the Court, subscribed £55 from their own pockets and guaranteed the same sum for the next two years for the maintenance of the technical education classes. This lavish subscription was continued by individual members of the Company for the next forty-five years. In 1896 the Master, John Coles, presented the Company with £100 to be invested in an annuity, the proceeds to go towards the expense of the Technical Education Class over the next ten years, and the Master in 1899, William Mann Cross, acknowledged Mr Coles' generous example and also gave £100 for the same purpose. When in 1896 the Court guaranteed the class £55 per annum for the next three years, there was only one dissentient, a Mr Baptie, who complained that it was not 'competent for the Court to bind the future action of individuals of the Court'.

The Technical Education Class Committee made annual reports to the Court. Thus in 1895:

> The Classes during the last year have been well attended. In the Autumn Term the class consisted of 10 students, being the full number that could be accomodated. The average attendance was 8.2. In the Winter Term the numbers fell off slightly during the severe weather during part of which unfortunately the heating apparatus was out of order. The average attendance was 7.5.
>
> In consequence of the demand made on us for accomodation, we made an application to the Carpenters Co who provided the class with additional space by enclosing a portion of the passage. This enabled your Committee to find room for 2 more benches (also kindly provided by the Carpenters Co.) & to increase the number of students to 14. In the Spring Term we again found no difficulty in getting students & soon filled up the full compliment of 14.
>
> During the course the students have been engaged on the following practical work:

A small cart body	Pair of shafts
Tail ladders	A front wheel
Under carriages	A Cart wheel

> and the component parts of vehicles: also morticing & tenoning, rebating &c. Several of the students have been engaged in drawing designs of different carts & wagons.

Your Committee early in the year decided to give the following prizes—one for 30/- & one for 20/- to which the Master, the Hon. A. de T. Egerton M.P. added an additional Prize of 20/- for merit in drawing. The prizes are to be given either in Books, Tools or Drawing Instruments. It was also decided to give Certificates of attendance to those attending two-thirds of the classes.

Your Committee visited the school at the close of last Term & allotted the Prizes as follows—

1st. W. Cox; 2nd. H. Spencer; The Master's Prize, W. Morgan. 7 certificates for attendance have also been awarded.

The Prizes & Certificates will be presented at Carpenters Hall (together with the Prizes given in other classes) in Decr. next.

The Donations given by Members of the Court have together with the fees sufficed to meet all the current expenses of the year, together with the additional expenditure for tools consequent upon the increase in the number of students.

In 1897 the Technical Education Committee reported:

That the classes during the past year have been well attended. The names of 19 students are on the register for the session or about 15 during each term with an average attendance each class night of 11 2/3rds—This is the highest we have yet obtained.

The practical work has been of a more advanced character than hitherto—it includes a van body—2 cart bodies—front & hind wheels—tailladders, front carriages &c. The technical drawings completed are very numerous & comprise almost every vehicle that is seen on the road.

At the present moment there are 5 or 6 students who have been in the class over 3 years; this fact shows that the students themselves appreciate the opportunity afforded them & are only too anxious to improve their knowledge of their own trade.

The Judges appointed by the Committee (Messrs. Saunders & Shepherd) awarded the following prizes which will be awarded at the Annual Distribution at Carpenters' Hall: First Prize 30/-, W. Cox; Second Prize 20/-, H. Spencer; & to E. Madden a Certificate of Merit. A Special Prize of £1.1.0 was given by the Worshipful Master (C. C. Paine Esq.) to A. D. Rawlings for merit in draughtsmanship.... Prizes of the value of £2.10 have also been offered to the class now opened at the Boro Polythechnic.

In the following summer the Court paid a special visit to the Wheelwrights' class-room and examined the work being done, and in 1899 the committee reported a record number of twenty-five students 'of ages from 13 to 49. Of these 21 are apprentices or improvers and there are 4 adults'.

The Rt Hon the Lord Mayor, Sir Ian Bowater, DSO, TD, opening an exhibition of the 'art and mistery' of the Wheelwright at the Guildhall Museum on 11 February 1970 with the Master, Dr G. S. Udall (centre) and the Upper Warden, H. S. Dodson (left)

In 1900 the Technical Education Committee recommended
that the Honorary Freedom of the Company should be given
to A. E. Garrod, who had won first prize in the Honours
Grade at City & Guilds of London Institute, and that the
expense of this should be borne by the technical education
fund. The Master, Francis Mercer, immediately offered to
defray the cost himself, but the Court ruled that it should come
out of the Company's general fund. Three years later it was
reported that eleven students had entered for the City &
Guilds Institute examination and all had passed, two taking
honours. 'Our students have taken the three highest prizes
offered.' A £5 5s course of lectures was started in 1904 'on the
elementary work of the motor car as applied to van building,
so as to bring the class up-to-date in all that appertains to the
work of a wheelwright'. This was found to be a great success
and was continued the following year.

Frank William Robson, who had been instructor to the
Wheelwrights' class since the scheme began, resigned in 1906
because the death of his father meant that he had to devote
more time to the family business. He was presented with a
testimonial (at a cost of four guineas) and was invited to the
Court Dinner to receive it. He was admitted to the Livery and
became Master of the Company in 1923.

P. W. Miller was appointed instructor in the lecturing and
drawing department at £7 a term, and B. Wallis as assistant
instructor in the practical department at £3 a term. In 1907
the committee reported that Mr Miller had taken a First Class
with Honours at the City & Guilds Institute, by whom he had
been registered as a teacher.

The class survived many difficulties; for instance, in 1912
'attendance fell off due mainly to a shortage of workmen in the
Trade, which caused a large amount of overtime to be worked';
but it continued throughout the First World War. The committee reported in 1915: 'The Wheelwrights' class has been
particularly affected by the war and in this respect probably
no class in the school has suffered more than ours'. Then in
1917: 'This class, although adversely affected by the demand

H

for war-work, has held its own in comparison with last year. The students are principally lads of 15 and 16 years of age, and show considerable interest in their work.' Frank Robson maintained his connection with the class by acting as one of the judges of work done, the other being Past Master William Shepherd.

When the Technical Education Committee appealed for funds in 1921, the Company voted £25 and three guineas towards a prize fund. Through the generosity of individual members of the Court and by occasional appeals to the Livery the class was kept going until the Second World War.

There were, of course, critics. In 1925 Mr C. Albert Paine, who had been admitted to the Livery in 1897, wrote asking why the Company did not enforce the apprenticeship system and spend more money on the Trade. The Clerk replied:

> There appears to be little prospect of any legislation with view to enforcing the apprenticeship system, having regard particularly to the attitude of the various Trade Unions on the subject; nor is it considered that the Wheelwrights Company, with its very limited means, can be expected to take a prominent lead in Trade matters.
>
> There is no income belonging to the Company available for such a purpose beyond the interest on a capital sum of £1,200, which is for the general purposes of the Company. As a matter of fact, the cost of maintaining the Wheelwrights' Class at the Trades Training Schools is actually paid out of a Fund to which each Member of the Court contributes.
>
> Beyond the Class to which I have referred, the Company has not been in direct touch with the Trade during the period you mention, viz., the last 25 years; but they communicate annually with the London firms of Wheelwrights and give particulars of the Company's Class for youths employed in the Trade.
>
> It is true that the Company gives a Livery Dinner each year and means are found for this purpose. Liverymen expect this function and without it our chances of obtaining new Liverymen would be materially reduced.
>
> The Accounts are laid before the Court each year, but are not circulated to the Livery.
>
> The Court Members take no fees and, with the exception of the Livery Dinner, the funds for the other functions are provided by the Master and Wardens.

In fact both Mr Paine and the Company were labouring to maintain an almost vanished tradition. Christopher Chataway

summed it up in a BBC television programme on 'The Wheel'
in November 1968:

> The wheelwright made wooden wheels for the first cars. His
> hammer became the power press of today, using a force of up to
> 600 pounds. The wheel is still made in separate sections: five opera-
> tions turn a flat steel disc into a modern wheel centre. The cart-
> wheel rim took days to shape. Steel rims are welded into a circle in
> seconds and pass through the shaping process automatically. The
> wheelwright had little enough help from machines. The steel disc
> and rim are assembled on a 40-ton press. Hand craft finally com-
> bined the sections of the wooden wheel. Today's automatic
> welder can complete 250 wheels an hour. One factory alone pro-
> duces 80,000 pressed steel wheels a week or four million a
> year. . . .

9

The Twentieth-Century Wheelwrights

A SPECIAL meeting of the Court was summoned on 24 February 1908 because of the sudden death of the Clerk, James Benjamin Scott, who had held office since 1870. The usual letters of condolence were sent, but the Court was obviously in great confusion. When in April it considered the duties and emoluments of the Clerk, difficulty arose 'as most of the information required was personal to the late Clerk and known only to him, but we have been assisted in our inquiries by his son, Mr Theodore James Scott'.

Indeed, Theodore Scott provided the Court with a two-page inventory of papers, books and plate, which were variously lodged in the Clerk's office at the Coal Exchange, the Coal Exchange strong room, and the Company's chest at Parr's Bank, 52 Threadneedle Street. He also put himself forward as a candidate for the Clerkship. There were four other applications and the Court selected three for election: Theodore Scott, T. Harvey Hull and J. L. Sayer. The last two had 'been in the Town Clerk's office at Guildhall for many years', and Theodore Scott was a solicitor. When it was put to the vote T. Harvey Hull was elected with twelve votes against Scott's four and Sayer's three. The salary reverted to £31 10s. Theodore Scott now pointed out that one-half of his late father's quarterly salary was still due, and the Court resolved that a full quarter's salary, £13 2s 6d, should be paid.

Thomas Harvey Hull was a worthy successor to James Benjamin Scott. He served in the office of Clerk for forty-one years until his death in 1949. He was admitted to the Livery in

1920 and served as Master in 1937. His long and devoted service to the Wheelwrights was only exceeded by his contemporary Beadle, James Smeed, who was Steward of the Guildhall Club when elected to succeed W. J. Baker in 1909. He was admitted Honorary Freeman of the Company in 1947, and continued in office until his death in 1957, when he was succeeded by his son, Mr Donald Smeed, the present Beadle at the time of writing.

In 1910 the Court recorded in the minutes their 'profound regret at the decease of His Majesty King Edward VII, an event which has plunged the whole civilised world into mourning and evoked from all classes of the community fervent expressions of loyalty and affection, which cannot fail to be consoling to the Royal Family'. The Company was represented at the memorial service for King Edward and at the service in St Pauls to celebrate the Coronation of King George V.

The First World War severely restricted the functions of the Company, and Colonel Thomas Horrocks Openshaw, CB, CMG, FRCS, who had been elected Master for the year 1915, held office for the unprecedented period of four years. He announced in January 1915 that as the expenses of the 1914 Master's Dinner had been less than usual the Master and Wardens would provide a sum of £40 to be divided between the Fund for the Relief of Officers' Families and the general fund of the Company.

There was no Livery Dinner in 1915, but in the following year the Company took part in the swearing-in ceremonies and the procession of the Lord Mayor, Colonel and Alderman Sir William Dunn, who was a Liveryman of the Wheelwrights. Six members of the Court went in two carriages in the Lord Mayor's procession, the horses being decorated with favours in the Company's heraldic colours of red and yellow. The Master wore his uniform and over it his official robe, the others wore their robes with black velvet Tudor caps. In July 1917 Sir William invited the Court to a luncheon at the Mansion House, 'and before proceedings terminated a warning was given of an impending German air raid. Some of the Members with the Right Honourable the Lord Mayor adjourned to the cellars under the Mansion House until the signal "all clear" was given by the Police.'

When in 1918 it was discovered that the Company had an overdraft of £200, members of the Court immediately collected £195 and the overdraft was cleared.

When Col Openshaw retired from office in 1918 the Court moved a special vote of thanks for 'his unprecedented four-year period of office as Master'. After expressing gratitude for his 'courtesy and hospitality' the minutes refer to him as a highly-skilled surgeon as well as an able organiser and administrator and go on to remark on his extraordinary success in founding Queen Mary's Hospital at Roehampton, 'an institution which derived some of its original impetus at a Dinner held under the auspices of the Company at Barbers Hall'. Openshaw was an outstanding orthopaedic surgeon and was senior surgeon at Queen Mary's Hospital as well as consulting surgeon to Eastern Command during the First World War; though there is no evidence that he was responsible for founding the hospital, he was one of the early workers and advisers there.

Immediately after the war the Company began to benefit from generous legacies of Past Masters. William Shepherd, who had been Master in 1894 left £2,000 on trust, the interest to be applied for the relief of the Company's pensioners. Lord Egerton of Tatton who, as the Hon Alan de Tatton Egerton, MP, had been Master in 1895, left £5,000 to the Company to be paid on the death of his wife, which did not occur until 1934.

Among the distinguished Masters who held office in the period between the two World Wars were Sir Kingsley Wood, MP, who later became Postmaster General, Minister of Health and Chancellor of the Exchequer; Sir Randle Holme, a President of the Law Society; Lord Ebbisham of Cobham, who was Lord Mayor of London in 1926; and Sir Sidney Fox, who was the Sheriff of London in 1952.

Shortly before the last war a minor scandal led the Company to consult the Court of Aldermen about its disciplinary powers over its members. In November 1935 the Court received a report about 'the disorderly conduct of a Liveryman who interrupted the speakers at a Livery Dinner in Grocers Hall'. The Clerk reported that he had discussed the affair in two interviews with the City Chamberlain, Sir Adrian Pollock. The offending Liveryman wrote a letter of apology but was summoned to appear before the Court. He did so, and admitted that there was no excuse for his behaviour, again apologising profusely, admitting that he was intoxicated and forgot himself. After some debate the Court decided to accept the apology and let the matter drop. The Master gave him a severe warning, expressing the hope that the Liveryman's future conduct would demonstrate his 'appreciation of the leniency shown by the Court. The Liveryman promised that his future conduct should reflect no discredit on the Company'.

Unfortunately, in October 1937 the Master reported a serious complaint by the Lord Mayor relating to the conduct of the same gentleman, 'one of the Livery, who addressed some very insulting remarks to Rt Hon E. Leslie Burgin, MP, the Minister of Transport, who was just leaving the building' after a Livery Dinner at the Mansion House. It was resolved that letters of apology should be sent to the Lord Mayor and to the Minister of Transport and that:

> The Liveryman be summoned before the Court and informed that his retirement from the Livery of the Company is insisted on, and further that this Court is taking action to exclude him forthwith from all future association with the Company, whose prestige has already suffered irreparable damage as the result of his disgraceful behaviour on this and on another occasion of public importance That the matter be brought to the notice of the Court of Aldermen, with a request that they will suggest what steps can be taken to expunge his name from the Roll of the Livery.

The Liveryman made a personal appearance before the Master and Wardens and promised to resign, but when his letter of resignation was received, 'it was qualified to such an extent as to be regarded as unsatisfactory'.

Meanwhile Sir Adrian Pollock, the Chamberlain, by instruction of the Court of Alderman, advised that the 'Court having the power to confer the Livery, has power also to take it away. As it is understood that the Liveryman concerned is about to tender his resignation, his name should merely be deleted from the Livery of the Company and will in due course cease to appear in the Common Hall Register'. The Chamberlain did, however, warn the Court on the resolution to exclude him from all future association with the Company:

> To give effect to such a Resolution would amount to disfranchise-ment from the Freedom of the Company. I am therefore desired to make it quite clear that although a Liveryman resigns from the Livery he still remains a Freeman of the Company and cannot be deprived of the customary rights and privileges that every Free-man possesses.

The Court thereupon resolved that the offender's name be deleted from the list of the Livery; that he be informed of this action; that the fees of £26 1s he paid on admission to the Livery in 1931 be returned; and that he be informed that his position as a Freeman was not affected.

The Second World War once again restricted the activities of the Company, but it did not follow the precedent of 1914–18. Masters and Wardens were elected annually. There was no Livery Dinner in 1939, but fifty guineas were given to the Mansion House Fund for the Red Cross & St John's War Organisation.

In January 1941 the Honorary Auditor, Past Master Charles Rooke, reported that he had

> examined the accounts of payments and receipts and that they were in order, but it was customary for a list of property, silver, records, etc. to be incorporated in the audit and it might be advisable to postpone the audit to ascertain the precise condition of such records, silver, etc. as those which had been stored at Guildhall could not be checked and examined for some time, being buried under debris.

In April, the Clerk reported that the records retrieved from the strong room at the Guildhall, scorched and wetted after enemy action, had been moved to the country.

> It is very satisfactory to be able to report that the Charter of Charles II and the Byelaws, all in their original cases, are safe

and in perfect condition, our Minute Books complete from 1766, and the Silver—part of which was buried for some months— complete and undamaged. It has now been deposited in a place of comparative safety outside London. A few of our earlier books have been burnt, but a great many of the papers were recovered and although damage by fire and water is apparent they are fairly complete. On the whole he thought that the Company had been fortunate, having suffered no serious losses except the early Minute Books, which had never been referred to during his Clerk-ship of 33 years.

For the historian, however, it was unfortunate, for the three minutes books covered the years 1670 to 1690, 1690 to 1725, and 1725 to 1766, the formative period of the Company.

The three keys of the Company's old oak chest, which had been in the bank for more than a century, were recovered from the Guildhall in a rusty condition, but were renovated at the expense of Past Master Victor Wilkins and were presented to the Court as 'interesting specimens of the locksmith's art in the seventeenth century'.

In 1943, when Mr Harvey W. L. Hull, the son of the Clerk, was admitted to the Livery, the Court resolved that because of the unpaid assistance he had given to his father and for his help in recovering the records of the Company from Guildhall the fees for admission to the Freedom and Livery be remitted. In the same year the Master, Wardens and some of the Assistants represented the Company at the first United Guilds Service at St Paul's Cathedral, and the Wheelwrights have since con-tinued to attend this annual Service.

With the end of the war in sight, the Wheelwrights could again look forward to expansion:

4th April, 1945
   A Letter from the Town Clerk stating that the Court of Alder-men have authorised an increase in the number of the Livery from 250 to 300 and setting the Livery Fine in future at a sum of not less than 50 guineas, was read, and the Clerk stated that the usual Fee, on an increase of Livery was £20, and was instructed to see that such Fee was duly paid to the Court of Aldermen.

The Court was also much exercised in the consideration of the principles of election and procedure. In 1949 it was re-solved that fifteen places (reduced to six in 1952) on the Court be kept for sons of Liverymen, persons taking up Livery by patrimony, or for distinguished or special persons; and in the same year:

> That the procedure for filling vacancies on the Court of Assistants in the future shall be based in general principle on seniority and shall be as follows:
>
> When a vacancy occurs, the Court shall instruct the Clerk to write to such Senior Liverymen, whom the Court may deem fit (after a ballot which shall be unanimous as to each name) to enquire whether such Liverymen would, if elected, be willing to serve on the Court. Should any such Liveryman, to whom the Clerk shall have written, state that he does not desire his name to be considered he shall be deemed to have declined permanently to offer himself for election to the Court, unless he shall request that consideration of his name shall be deferred to some later date for a reason which the Court regards as good and sufficient
>
> Provided always that the Court shall not be precluded from inviting Liverymen out of seniority to be considered for election to the Court, having regard to any special qualifications they may have or any particular service they may have rendered to the community or to the Company or for any other reason.

Thus, after more than a century the principle of seniority was definitely approved by the Court. Five years later more detailed procedure for the election of Assistants was drawn up. On 28 January 1954 the Court resolved:

> (a) This Court is satisfied with the Resolution of the Court of 6th July 1949 as constituting the principles governing election to the Court save that instead of the words '(after a ballot which shall be unanimous as to each name)' there shall be substituted the words '(after a ballot indicating approval by a majority as to each name of not less than three fourths of such members of the Court as vote at the Court meeting at which the names are considered)'
>
> (b) Subject to compliance with the Resolution of 6th July 1949 (with the said amendment) the following procedure shall be adopted in relation to election of Assistants:
>
> (1) That each candidate through seniority shall be required to complete a pro forma to be sent to him by the Clerk and thereafter to attend before a meeting of a committee consisting of the Master and Wardens for the time being, two Past Masters and one Assistant who has not passed the Chair
>
> (2) Such Committee shall thereafter submit the name of each candidate considered by them to the Court together with the committee's recommendations thereon and if such nomination

shall then be approved by not less than three fourths of the members of the Court present and voting the candidate shall be deemed to be duly elected

(3) With regard to nominations of Liverymen out of seniority such nominations shall be made on a pro forma and shall be signed by not less than four members of the Court. Each such nomination shall be placed before the Court and if the Court approves the nomination being considered (after a ballot indicating the approval of a majority of not less than three fourths of such members of the Court as vote thereon) the nomination shall be submitted to the said Committee for consideration, interview of the nominee and report to the Court together with the Committee's recommendations thereon for determination by the Court in the same manner as is applicable to other nominations for the Court.

(4) The foregoing procedure shall be applicable to any Liverymen who shall have already indicated their willingness to serve on the Court if elected, and as regards nominations received pursuant to the Resolution of 16th July 1953 these shall not be deemed to be in nomination pending compliance with such procedure recommended

(5) In consequence the provision of the Resolution of 15th January, 1953 that

> Before filling any vacancy on the Court Liverymen who have indicated willingness to serve if elected should be invited to meet the Court shall be and is hereby rescinded.

Pro forma for Candidature for the Court of Assistants
> Name of Liveryman
> Address
> Date of Birth
> Date of admission to the Livery
> Whether son of a Liveryman &
> if so name of Father
> Whether otherwise related to any past or
> present Liveryman and if so, the relationship
> Full particulars of occupation
> Decorations, Honours etc.
> Particulars of any public service
> or special qualification
> Whether ever insolvent
> Signature
> Date

NB—Instead of signature by the Candidate the following to be substituted on pro formas for use in cases of nomination other than through seniority:

> We desire consideration by the Court of above named gentleman as a Candidate for the Court, and from our own

knowledge of him recommend him as in every respect a
fit and proper person to serve on the Court.

(To be signed by four members of the Court)

The earliest representation of the Wheelwright's Coat-of-Arms dates from 1682. They appear on the Poor's Box in iron, painted in heraldic colours. But the Company was in for a surprise.

8th February, 1950

The Court then proceeded agreeably to the item on the Agenda to consider an application by Messrs. E. H. Kelsey Ltd. Brewers, to incorporate the Arms of the Wheelwrights Company on an Inn Sign at Matfield, Kent. A considerable discussion ensued as to the desirability of giving the sanction sought by the Brewers. It was eventually proposed that the application be refused. An amendment was put forward that the matter be postponed for further consideration and the Clerk be instructed to make further relevant enquiries.

On the matter being put to the vote there were nine in favour of the amendment and eight to the contrary and the matter was accordingly referred to the Clerk for further enquiries.

At the next Court the Clerk reported that 'the College of Arms had informed him that no Grant of Arms had been made to the Company and that, therefore, the Company had no coat-of-arms and were not in a position to grant any use of it or otherwise'.

It was then resolved that Messrs Kelsey be informed that the Court had no objection to the use of its coat-of-arms on the inn sign, subject to the Court's prior approval of the design proposed. But the Company decided not to apply to the College of Arms for a grant. However, in 1962 the matter was revived, and the Court eventually agreed to apply for a Grant of Arms and Supporters at a cost of £345. It was decided that the cost should not be borne by the Company's funds, but by subscriptions from members of the Court.

After some lengthy negotiations between Past Master Leonard Norris and Portcullis Pursuivant, who insisted that there should be some differentiation of the supporters, the design was finally agreed by the Company and approved by the Kings of Arms. The Letters Patent were received in 1965. The blazon of the armorial bearings, which differ only in details from that used by the Company since its foundation is:

ARMS: Gules a chevron between three wheels Or on a chief Argent a broad axe blade to the sinister proper.

CREST: On a wreath Argent and Gules a dexter arm embowed vested Azure cuffed Argent the hand proper holding a mallet Or.

SUPPORTERS: On either side a horse Argent each gorged with a circlet pendent therefrom over the foreleg a chain terminated by a ring Or.

MOTTO: God Grant Unity.

So at long last the Company obtained official recognition of, and rights over, its coat-of-arms; but the origin of the seventeenth-century armorial bearings remains a mystery.

Strenuous efforts were made to revive the Company's connection with the Trade in the post-war period, but the Trade had almost vanished. A new Technical Education Committee was formed in 1950 and in the following year Certificates of Merit were awarded for wheel-making exhibits at the Royal Agricultural Show. No amount of generous intentions could re-create the ancient craft, so in 1966 it was resolved that the Company should become a Founding Subscription Member of the City & Guilds of London Institute, paying fifty guineas a year under deed of covenant. It was also decided to give an annual prize of ten guineas, with a certificate or medal, to the winner of the City & Guilds' award for the new Vehicle Body Engineering Technician's Certificate. The Company has, in addition, given prizes to the Polytechnic Craft Schools and the City of London School.

Although the members of the Company are not confined to any religious denomination, it was thought appropriate that the Wheelwrights, like a number of other Livery Companies, should have the services of a Chaplain. So in 1954, the Rev Canon Richard Stafford Morris, MA, RD, a Liveryman of the Company, was appointed as Honorary Chaplain. Canon Morris died in 1961, and in 1968 the Rev Dr B. A. C. Kirk-Duncan, MA (Oxon), MA, PhD (TCD), Rector of St Mary-at-Hill, Eastcheap, was appointed to the office.

In the past twelve years there has been a great deal of tidying up in Company usage and procedure, bringing both more into line with the original provisions of the Charter and Bylaws. For instance, in 1958 it was resolved: 'That the terms *Upper Warden* and *Renter Warden* should henceforth *always be used* to designate the Wardens, and the terms Senior Warden and Junior Warden discontinued for all purposes'.

In 1967, after the Clerk had presented an analysis of attendance by Members of the Court of Assistants, it was resolved to revive and enforce the ancient bylaw by which Assistants could be fined for non-attendance at Court meetings. The Court decided: 'That a fine of one guinea be imposed on any Assistant for non-attendance, unless leave of absence be granted by the Master. Such leave of absence to be given at the Master's discretion in the case of illness, business or other excusable matters, but not including holidays'.

The Court's chief concern, however, was the same as it had been during its early beginnings, that of finance. Although many Past Masters had made generous donations and bequests and Members of the Court voluntarily met a number of expenses, there remains a continuous struggle against rising costs. The fine for admission to the Livery by Redemption has been increased by stages from fifty guineas to one hundred and fifty guineas, and the Court fine for an Assistant, which stood at £50 in 1900 was raised to £100 and then in 1967 to £150. Dining fees for Liverymen and their guests have also been increased. An appeal for funds to the Livery, launched with most generous subscriptions by members of the Court, was made at the end of 1961 and had produced more than £4,140 by 1965. In 1969 a further appeal for a Tercentenary Fund was made. In 1967 it was resolved, after a long debate, that quarterage, which had first been compounded at £2 in 1890 and then at £5 in 1908, should be charged annually to new Liverymen in the sum of six guineas. It was then found that this reversal to ancient custom at an increased rate would require the approval of the Court of Aldermen, so the Company petitioned in time-honoured form:

To: The Right Honourable the Lord Mayor and
   Court of Aldermen of the City of London

> The Petition
> of the Master, Wardens and Court of Assistants of the
> Worshipful Company of Wheelwrights of the City of
> London
> Sheweth:

That the present Ordinances of the Company came into force
on 2nd October, 1713, when Her Majesty Queen Anne laid down
Ordinances under the Charter of the Company, granted on 3rd
February, 1670, which Charter and Ordinances were ordered to be
enrolled among the Records of the City by your Honourable
Court on 7th December, 1773, when granting a Livery to the
Company

That the Ordinances provide (inter alia) for the payment by
Members of the Company of Quarterage at the rate of not more
than twelve pence per quarter which is no longer an adequate
rate of contribution towards the Charges of the Company

That your Petitioners have therefore resolved to amend the
Ordinances so as to provide in future for the payment of Quarterage at a rate adequate to the needs of the times

That your Petitioners have accordingly made the following
Ordinance in substitution for the present Ordinance relating to
Quarterage, viz.:—

> It shall be lawful for the Master, Wardens and Assistants
> for the time being by their Officers to levy collect and
> receive of the Members of the Company a competent
> sum of money to be by them agreed from time to time
> by the name of Quarterage towards the charges of the
> Company.

Your Petitioners therefore humbly pray that your Honourable
Court will be pleased to approve the amended Ordinance in the
form set out above and order that it be enrolled among the
Records of the City of London

And your Petitioners will ever pray &c.

Signed by the Master	F. Griffiths Woollard	
and Wardens and the		Master
Clerk in accordance	R. E. Stubington ⎱	Wardens
with a Resolution passed	Dr. G. S. Udall ⎰	
at a Court of Assistants	M. H. Hinton	Clerk
held on the twenty sixth		
day of June, 1968.		

Presented by H. Murray Fox, Alderman.

On 15 October 1968 the Court of Aldermen approved the

recommendation that 'the prayer of the Petition be complied with, and the amendment to the Ordinance sanctioned accordingly, subject to the condition that if it is allowed by the Privy Council it shall be enrolled among the records of the City. . . .' And so, after three centuries, with the revival of one of its oldest bylaws, the Wheelwrights' wheel has turned full circle.

As this brief history shows, the Company has indeed for three centuries preserved its traditions and pursued the objectives for which it was founded, as far as changing conditions have allowed.

With no Trade to regulate, the Company has made generous use of its limited funds to further technical education and keep alive the spirit of craftsmanship.

Members of the Court have even sought out and collected a number of old wheelwrights' implements, but strenuous efforts to turn a permanent exhibition into a wheelwrights' museum have so far been frustrated. However, through the good offices of an Assistant, a selection of wheelwrights' tools was sent for exhibition at the British Week in Tokyo in 1969 and a further exhibition is being mounted at the Guildhall Museum in 1970, the Tercentenary Year.

Apprentices are still bound to Liverymen of the Company, though not, of course, as wheelwrights, and after serving their time are eligible for the Freedom. The Company's reputation for hospitality and sociability has remained unscathed through all the financial vicissitudes of the centuries. So, too, has the tradition of the Poor's Box, and the Court awards regular pensions to dependants of Liverymen who are in need.

Quietly and unobtrusively Members of the Court and Livery give generously of time and money to preserve both the Company and its future prestige, and in the Tercentenary Year still wider uses of its funds for charitable purposes are being explored. The Wheelwrights enter their fourth century as 'one Body Corporate and Politique in deede and name', old in

Group at the tercentenary livery banquet of the Company, held at Stationers' Hall on 3 February 1970: (*from left to right*) Alderman and Sheriff, the Rt Hon Lord Mais; the Archdeacon of London; M. H. Hinton, the Clerk; H. S. Dodson, the Upper Warden; the Rt Hon the Lord Mayor, Sir Ian Bowater; Dr G. S. Udall, the Master; D. F. Smeed, the Beadle; the Rt Rev the Lord Bishop of Norwich; D. T. Russell, the Renter Warden; the Rev Dr B. A. C. Kirk-Duncan, the Honorary Chaplain; Mr Sheriff R. Theodore Beck

The Rt Hon the Lord Mayor being welcomed by the Master, Dr G. S. Udall, to the tercentenary dinner at Stationers' Hall on 3 February 1970

tradition, but ever new in the spirit of progress, enterprise and brotherhood, which makes that tradition a vital part of civic life today.

APPENDIX I

The Charter Granted to the Wheelwrights by King Charles II, 3 February 1670

CHARLES THE SECOND By the Grace of God King of England Scotland France and Ireland Defender of the Faith &c. TO ALL to whome these presents shall come GREETING

WHEREAS WEE are informed by the humble Peticion of divers Wheelewrightes in and neere the Citty of London that certaine Forreigners undertake the profession and trade of a Wheelewright notwithstanding they are ignorant and unskillfull therein and altogether uncapable of makeing the worke used in and about the said Citty whereby much mischeife happneth to persons in the Street by falling of Cartes and Coaches and great damage to Merchants and others in theire Goodes as aloee losse and danger to Gentlemen occasioned by the ignorance and ill worke of the said forreigners that never served to the said profession and other great inconveniences and misdemeanours used and practized in the said Arte and trade for the prevencion whereof WEE have beene humbly besought to Incorporate them into a Body Politique and to invest them with such priviledges and powers as may bee meete and necessary for the well ordering and regulateing of the same Art and Mistery

NOW KNOW YEE that WEE taking the premisses into our princely consideracion and being desirous to advance the good and benefitt of the Artistes and Freemen of the said Art and Mistery and for the generall good and advantage of all our loveing Subjectes of our especiall grace certaine knowledge and meere mocion HAVE ordeyned granted and constituted and appointed And by these presentes for us our Successors DOE ordeyne grant constitute and appoint that MATHEW BATEMAN ESQUIRE RALPH ASHBY FRANCIS JESSON RICHARD SMART CHRISTOPHER HAWES BARTHOLOMEW HOOPER RICHARD BURGIS WILLIAM DUKE JOHN TURNER SAMUELL GAYNES WILLIAM CRADOCKE JOHN EADES RICHARD MERRITT JOHN SLADE JOHN BOX ROBERT TAVERNER WILLIAM LAWTON JAMES WYNNE JOHN PRESTON EDWARD WRIGHT AND BENJAMIN PHILLIPES Cittizens of London being all Wheelewrightes and Freemen of the said Citty of London and all such other person and persons as now doe or hereafter shall or may use the said Art of Mistery of Wheelewrights within the said Citty of London and five myles compasse thereof for ever hereafter bee and shall bee by vertue of these presentes one Body Corporate and Politique in deede and in name and shall have contynuance and per-

130

petuall succession for ever by the name of Master Wardens Assistantes and Commonalty of the Arte and Mistery of Wheelewrightes of the Citty of London

And that they and theire successors shall be for ever hereafter persons able and capable in the Law to purchase have receive and enjoy Mannors Landes Tenementes liberties priviledges Jurisdiccions Franchises and other hereditaments whatsoever of what kind nature or quality soever thay bee to them and theire Successors in Fee and Perpetuity or for terme of life lives or yeares or otherwise in what sort soever they bee soe as the same exceede not the cleare yearely value of forty pounds the Statute of Mortmaine or anything therein conteyned or any other Act or Statute to the contrary notwithstanding

And alsoe all manner of Goodes chattells and things whatsoever of what name nature or quality soever they bee and alsoe to give grant sett assigne alien sett over and dispose of any the said Mannors Messuages Landes Tenementes & hereditamentes Goodes and Chattells at theire wills and pleasures

And that they and theire Successors by that name shall and may bee able to plead and bee impleaded answeare and bee answeared defend and bee defended in what Court or Courts soever and before any Judge or Justice and other persons and Officers of us and our successors whatsoever in all and singular Accions Pleas suites Plaintes matters and demands of what kind quality or sort soever

And alsoe to doe performe and execute all such Actes and things whatsoever as fully and amply to all intentes and purposes as any other Bodyes Politique or Corporate within this our Kingdome of England or Dominion of Wales can or may act or doe

AND FURTHER That they the said Master Wardens Assistantes and Commonalty of the Art and Mistery of Wheelewrightes in the Citty of London and their successors shall and may for ever hereafter have a Common Seale to serve and use in and for all causes matters and affaires whatsoever of them and theire successors and that itt shall and may bee lawfull to and for them and theire successors to breake alter and make new the said Seale from tyme to tyme at theire wills and pleasures

AND FURTHER WEE WILL and ordeyne And by these presentes for us and our successors DOE give and grante unto the said Master Wardens Assistantes and Commonalty and theire successors for the tyme being full power and authority to assemble themselves and meete together from tyme to tyme in some convenient place within the said Citty of London where they shall thinke most

And then and there they shall and may elect and choose of the said Art and Mistery in manner and forme hereafter in these presentes mencioned a meete person who shall and may bee called the Master of the said Company And alsoe then and there elect and choose two other of the said Company in manner and forme herafter mencioned who shall bee and shall bee called the Wardens of the said Company And also then and there nominate eighteene other meete persons of the said Society in manner and forme hereafter in these presentes expressed who shall bee and shall bee called the Assistantes of the said Company who from tyme to tyme shall be ayding and assisting to the said Master and Wardens for the tyme being in all causes matters and thinges touching or concerning the said Company

And alsoe that the said Master Wardens and Assistantes and theire Successors for the tyme being or any five or more of them haveing obteyned a warrant from the Lord Cheife Justice of the Court of Kinges Bench for the tyme being and with the assistance of a Constable or any other lawfull Officer shall have full power and authority from tyme to tyme and at all convenient tymes peceably and quietly to enter into the House Shopp yard or Warehouse of any Member of the said Society or other persons employed by him there to search prove try and see whether the wheeles and Goodes made sold or put to sale or offered to bee made sold or putt to sale by him or them bee made of good and sufficient materialls and well and duely made and wrought and such as shall bee found not to bee made of good materialls and well and duely made and wrought to seize upon and carry away to the end the same may be duely examined and tryed by the said Master Wardens and Assistantes or the major part of them and disposed of according to Lawe

AND FURTHER WEE DOE Grant for us and our Successors by these presentes unto the said Master Wardens Assistantes and Commonaltie of the Art and Mistery of Wheelewrightes of the Citty of London for the tyme being that they or the greater part of them Whereof the Master and one of the Wardens aforesaid for the tyme being to bee two shall and may have full power and authority be vertue of these presentes to make ordeyne constitute appoint and sett downe from tyme to tyme such reasonable Lawes Actes Orders Ordinances and Constitucions in writing as to them or the greater part of them whereof the Master and one of the Wardens as aforesaid for the tyme being to bee two shall seeme good fitt and convenient according to their best discretion as well for and concerning such fitt and legall Oathes as shall be requisite to bee administred to the Master Wardens and Assistantes or any other of the said Society for touching and concerneing the good rule and Government of the said Company or any the Members thereof as for the punishment and reformacion of such deceiptes and abuses as shall from tyme to tyme bee practized either in uttering or making bad and deceiptfull Wheeles and Goodes by any Member of the said Society or any other imployed by him within the said Citty of London or any other place or places within the lymittes aforesaid

And also to provide and lymitt such reasonable paines penaltyes and punishments either by Fynes Amerciamentes or any other lawfull wayes or meanes whatsoever upon all Offenders or breakers of such Actes Orders Ordinances and Constitucions as to the said Master Wardens and Assistantes or any five or more of them whereof the Master and one the Wardens to bee two shall thinke fitt

And that the said Master Warden Assistantes and Commonalty and theire Successors shall and may by vertue of these presentes have and take the same by distress Accion of Debt or other lawfull wayes or meanes whatsoever the said Fynes and Amerciamentes to bee and remaine to the use of the said Society and theire Successors without the giveing or rendring any Accompt or other thinge to us or our Successors in that behalfe

All which Actes Ordinances and Constitucions soe as aforesaid to bee made WEE WILL shall bee observed obeyed performed and kept under the paines and penaltyes therein to bee conteyned soe as alwayes such Actes Ordinances Constitucions Fynes and Amerciamentes bee reasonable and not repugnant or contrary but as neere as may bee agreeable to the Lawes and Statutes of this Kingdome and to the Custome or usage of our said Citty of London

AND FURTHER for the better Execucion of this our Grant WEE HAVE created assigned named constituted and made And by these presentes for us and our Successors DOE create assign name constitute make and appoint the said MATHEW BATEMEN to bee the first and present Master of the said Company Who shall contynue in the said Office from the date of these presentes untill the Thursday next following the Nyne and twentieth day of September now next comeing if he shall soe long live and well behave himselfe in the said Office and from thenceforth untill one other of the said Society shall bee chosen and sworne into the said Office of Master in due manner according to the Ordinances and provisions in that behalfe in these presentes mencioned and expressed Hee the said MATHEW BATEMAN takeing his Corporall Oath before the Lord Mayor of our Citty of London for the tyme being for the due and faithfull execucion of the said Office or place TO which said Lord Mayor WEE DOE hereby for us and our Successors give power and authority to administer and give the said Oath to the said MATHEW BATEMAN accordingly

AND ALSOE WEE HAVE ASSIGNED named Constituted and made And by these presentes for us and our Successors DOE ASSIGNE name ordeyne constitute and make the said RALPH ASHBY and FRANCIS JESSON to bee the first and present wardens of the said Company And that they and either of them respectively shall continue in the said Office from the day of the date of these presentes untill the said Thursday next following the aforesaid Nyne and twentieth day of September now next comeing if the said RALPH ASHBY and FRANCIS JESSON or either of them respectively shall soe long live and shall well demeane themselves in theire said Offices or places respectively and from thenceforth untill two others of the said Society shall bee duely chosen and sworne unto the said Office of Wardens of the said Company according to the Ordinances and Provisions herein expressed and declared They the said RALPH ASHBY and FRANCIS JESSON takeing theire respective Corporall Oathes before the said MATHEW BATEMAN whome wee doe hereby authorize to administer the said Oath to each of them accordingly

AND WEE LIKEWISE HAVE ASSIGNED named constituted appointed and made and by these presentes for us and our Successors DOE ASSIGNE name and constitute and make the said RICHARD SMART CHRISTOPHER HAWES BARTHOLOMEW HOOPER RICHARD BURGES WILLIAM DUKE JOHN TURNER SAMUELL GAMES WILLIAM CRADOCKE JOHN EADES RICHARD MERRITT JOHN SLADE JOHN BOX ROBERT TAVERNER WILLIAM LAWTON JAMES WYNN JOHN PRESTON EDWARD WRIGHT and BENJAMINE PHILLIPES to bee the first and present Assistantes of the said Company whome wee will shall continue in the said Office of Assistantes dureing theire Naturall lives unlesse they or any of them respectively shall bee removed for misbehaving of themselves in theire said Office or for some other just and reasonable cause they and every of them takeing their respective Corporall Oathes before the said MATHEW BATEMAN Master of the said Society for the faithfull execucion of their said place of Assistantes whome wee doe hereby authorize to administer the same Oath accordingly

AND WEE WILL and by these presentes for us and our Successors DOE GRANT unto the said Master Wardens Assistantes and Commonalty of the said Art and Mistery of wheelewrightes of the Citty of London and theire Successors That the said Master Wardens and Assistants of the said Company for the tyme being or the greater part of them whereof wee will that the Master and one of the Wardens for the tyme being to bee two from tyme to tyme for ever hereafter shall have full power and authority yearely and every yeare at and upon the Thursday next following the Nyne and twentieth day of September to elect and nominate one of the Wardens or Assistantes for the tyme being to bee the Master of the said Company for one whole yeare thence next ensueing and untill one other of the said Wardens or Assistantes shall bee elected and sworne according to the Ordinances and Provisions of these presentes expressed and declared

And that such persons as shall bee soe chosen and named unto the said Office of Master of the said Company before he bee admitted to execute the same shall take his Corporall Oath before the said last preceedent Master and Wardens of the said Company or any two of them And before the Assistantes for the tyme being or the greater part of them to execute the said Office rightly well and faithfully in all thinges touching the same And that after such Oath soe as aforesaid taken shall have and execute the said Office for one whole yeare from thence next ensueing and untill one other shall be duely elected and chosen in his place or stead according to the provisions in these presentes conteyned to which last preceedent Master and Wardens for the tyme being or any two of them Wee by these presentes for us our heires and Successors DOE give and grant full power and authority from tyme to tyme to administer the said Oath accordingly

And likewise that at the same tyme of electing the said Master as aforesaid The said Master Wardens and Assistantes of the said Company for the tyme being or the greater part of them whereof the Master and one of the Wardens for the tyme being to bee two shall and may alsoe elect choose and nominate two other of the Assistantes of the said Society who shall bee and shall bee called the Wardens of the said Company for one whole yeare thence next ensueing and untill two others of the said Assistantes bee duely chosen elected and sworne unto the said Office of Wardens of the said Company according to the Ordinances provisions herein after declared and expressed

And that such persons as shall be soe chosen and named unto the said Office of Wardens of the said Company before they bee admitted to execute the same shall take theire respective Corporall Oathes before the last preceedent Master and Wardens of the said Company or any two of them for the tyme being well and duely to execute theire Office in all thinges touching the same and that after such Oathes soe as aforesaid taken the said persons shall and may execute their said Offices for one whole year from thence next ensueing and untill two others shall bee duely Elected and chosen in their places and steads according to the provisions in these presentes conteyned to which said last preceedent Master and Wardens or any two of them for the tyme being WEE by these presentes for us and our Successors

DOE GRANT to the aforesaid Master Wardens Assistantes and Commonalty of the Art and Mistery of the Wheelewrightes of the Citty of London and theire Successors that if the Master and the Wardens of the said Company now and for the tyme being or any of them at any time after they shall bee elected and chosen into his or theire Office or Offices shall happen to dye or bee removed from his or theire said Office or Offices which said Master and Wardens and every of them for ill Government or for any other just and reasonable cause WEE WILL from tyme to tyme shall be removed by the greatest part of the Master Wardens and Assistantes of the Company aforesaid for the tyme being that then and soe often in any of those cases itt shall and may bee lawfull to and for the said Master Wardens and Assistantes for the tyme being or the greater part of them at theire wills and pleasures one other or others of the Assistantes aforesaid to bee Master or Wardens of the said Company in the place or places of him or them soe deceased or removed to elect and choose according to the Orders and Provisions before in these presentes expressed and declared to execute and exercize the said Office of Master Warden or Wardens of the said Company untill the Thursday after the Nyne and twentieth day of September then next following and then and from thenceforth untill some other meete person or persons shall bee elected and sworne to bee Master and Wardens of the said Company respectively as aforesaid

NEVERTHELESS WEE WILL that every Master and Warden of the said Society to bee nominated and elected in the place or places of him or them soe dyeing or being removed from tyme to tyme for ever before he shall be admitted to the execucion of the said Office shall take his Corporall Oath before the Master Wardens and Assistantes for the tyme being or the greater part of them well rightly and faithfully to execute the said Office in and by all thinges respectively touching and concerneing the same to which said Master Wardens and Assistantes for the tyme being or the greater part of them WEE DOE by these presentes for us our heires and Successors GIVE AND GRANT full power and authority from tyme to tyme as occasion shall require to administer such Oath and Oathes accordingly

AND FURTHER WEE WILL and by these presentes for us our heires and Successors DOE GRANT to the aforesaid Master Wardens Assistantes and Commonalty of the Art and Mistery of Wheelewrightes of the Citty of London and theire Successors that whensoever itt shall happen any of the Assistantes of the said Company now and for the tyme being to dye or bee removed from his said Office which said Assistantes and every of them for evill government or for any just and reasonable cause WEE WILL from tyme to tyme bee removed by the greater part of the Master Wardens and Assistantes of the Art and Mistery aforesaid for the tyme being That then and soe often it shall and may bee lawfull to and for the said Master Wardens and Assistantes for the tyme being or the greater part of them at theire wills and pleasures to elect and ordeyne one other or others of the said Society being meete person or persons to bee Assistant or Assistantes in the place or places of him or them deceased or removed according to the Orders and provisions before in these presentes expressed and declared to execute and exercize the said Office of Assistant or Assistantes dureing his or theire Naturall life or lives in manner and forme aforesaid

NEVERTHELESS WEE WILL that every Assistant of the said Society soe to be nominated and elected in the place or places of him or them soe dying or removed shall from tyme to tyme before he or they bee admitted to the Execution of his Office of Assistant take his or theire Corporall Oath before the Master and Wardens for the tyme being or any two of them to whome by these presentes WEE give power and authority to administer the said Oath accordingly and soe often as the cause shall require

AND ALSOE WEE WILL and by these presentes for us our heires and Successors DOE GRANT unto the said Master Wardens Assistantes and Commonalty and theire Successors full power and authority That the Master Wardens and Assistantes of the said Company for the tyme being or the greater part of them shall and may from tyme to tyme nominate elect choose and constitute one fitt and meete person to bee Clerke of the said Company to serve for the affaires of the said Society and to allow him such Sallary as they shall thinke fitt and one other fitt and meete person to bee Beadle of the said Company to be serviceable and attendant on the said Master Wardens and Assistantes of the said Company and all matters touching the same and to allow him such Sallary as they shall thinke fitt and the said Clerke and Beadle and either of them for reasonable or just cause to displace and remove and other persons in theire place or places at the discrecion of the Master Wardens and Assistantes or the greater part of them for the time being to choose and elect which said Clerke and Beadle soe elected and ordeyned before they bee admitted to the execucion of theire said Offices shall take their Corporall Oathes before the Master Wardens and Assistantes of the said Society for the tyme being or the greater part of them well faithfully and honestly to demeane and behave themselves in the execucion of the said Offices respectively to which said Master Wardens and Assistantes or the greater part of them for the tyme being for us our heires and Sucessors WE DOE hereby give powere and authority to administer such like Oathes as well to the aforesaid Clerke and Beadle as to all other persons which from tyme to tyme shall be admitted into the said Society

AND WEE DOE hereby nominate and appoint THOMAS JOHNSON Gentleman to bee the first Clerke and HENRY FOTHERINGHAM the first Beadle both to bee sworne according to the power and authority in that behalfe herein before expressed

And for the better discovery of the false deceiptfull and insufficient Workes belonging to the saide Arte or Trade WEE WILL and by these presentes for us our heires and Successors DOE ordeyne and firmely charge and Command that noe person or persons whatsoever from henceforth within the said Citty of London and five miles compasse of the same doe use exercize or practize the said Art or Mistery of Wheelewright unlesse hee or they shall first have served as an Apprentice or Apprentices for the space of seaven yeares at the least to a Freeman of the said Company or some other person or persons lawfully useing or exercizing the said Art or Mistery of Wheelewright according to the Statute in that behalfe made and provided upon paine of being proceeded against for his or theire contemptes thereof according to the lawes and Statues of this our Realme

AND WEE well weighing and considering the good order and honest practice of the Art or Mistery aforesaid will conduce much to the benefitt and good of the people of this Kingdome and that the Members thereof being under the Government of the Citty of London the Offenders in the said Trade are like to bee more effectually dealt withall and punished according to theire demerittes And those that doe use and exercize the same as they ought to doe the better comforted and encouraged

WEE HEREBY DECLARE our will and pleasure to bee That the Lord Mayor and Aldermen of the Citty of London for the tyme being doe cause and allow these our Letters Patent to bee Inrolled within the Common Chamber of the same Citty amongst the Recordes thereof to the intent that those that are and shall bee Freemen of London and Members of the said Society of Wheelewrightes may bee subject to the government of the said Citty and may enjoy the benefitt thereof

AND FURTHER WEE WILL ordeyne and Grant for us our heires and Successors by these presentes to the said Master Wardens Assistantes and Commonalty of the Art and Mistery of Wheelewrightes of the Citty of London and theire Successors that itt shall and may bee lawfull to and for the said Master Wardens and Assistantes or the greater part of them for the tyme being to take in and admitt into the same Society such person and persons as they shall from tyme to tyme thinke fitt and as shall desire to become Members of the said Society and to administer such legall and fit Oath or Oathes unto them as to the Freemen of the said Society are or shall bee usually administered

AND FURTHERMORE WEE WILL by these presentes for us and our Successors DOE firmely charge and command all and singular Justices of the peace Mayors Sheriffes Bayliffes Constables and other Officers and Ministers of us and our heires and Successors to whom it shall apperteyne that from tyme to tyme they shall bee and shall bee ayding and assisting to the aforesaid Master and Wardens and Assistantes for the tyme being and the Deputy and Deputyes of the said Master and Wardens for the tyme being respectively whome wee doe hereby give full power and authority to make and constitute under the Seale of the said Company with full power and authority to make search and act and doe all thinges in theire places and steades as full and amply as they may respectively doe or performe by vertue of and according to the intent of these presentes in the due execucion of these our Letters Patentes in and by all thinges to the true intent and meaning thereof

AND MOREOVER WEE WILL and by these presentes for us and our Successors DOE GRANT to the aforesaid Master Wardens and Society and theire Successors That these our Letters Patentes or the Inrollment of the same and all and singular matters and thinges in the same conteyned from tyme to tyme shall be good sufficient firme and effectuall in the Law in all thinges according to the true intent hereof and shall bee expounded and construed cheifely beneficially and largely for the greatest profitt benefitt and advantage of the aforesaid Masters Wardens and Society and their Successors

PROVIDED ALWAYES that if itt shall at any tyme hereafter bee made appeare to us our heires or Successors That these our Letters Pantentes of Incorporacion or any the Causes powers or priviledges thereby granted are prejudiciall or inconvenient or not of publique use and benefitt then upon significacion or Declaracion thereof to bee made by us our heires or Successors under our or theire Signett Signe Manuall or Privy Seale These presentes or such or soe many of the said powers and priviledges whereof any such significacion or Declaracion shall bee soe made shall from thenceforth cease determyne and have noe longer being Anything therein conteyned to the contrary thereof notwithstanding

PROVIDED FURTHER And our will and pleasure is That the Master Wardens and Assistantes of the said Company for the tyme being and all other person or persons to bee from tyme to tyme admitted into the said Society shall before they enter upon the execucion of theire respective Offices or places or become Members of the said Fellowship by admittance thereunto shall severally take the Oathes of ALLEGIANCE and SUPREMACY before the Master and Wardens for the tyme being or two of them whereof the Master to bee one to whome wee doe hereby give full power and authority to administer the same Oathes accordingly

ALTHOUGH EXPRESSE MENCION of the true yearely value or certainty of the premisses or any of them or of any other Guiftes or Grantes by us or by any of our Progenitors or Predecessors heretofore made to the said Master Wardens Assistantes and Commonalty of Wheelewrightes of the Citty of London and theire Successors in these presentes is not made or any Statute Act Ordinance Provision Proclamacion or Restriccion heretofore had made enacted ordeyned or provided or any other matter cause or thing whatsoever to the contrary thereof notwithstanding IN WITNES whereof wee have caused these our Letters to bee made Patentes WITNES OUR SELFE at Westminster the Third day of February in the two and twentieth yeare of our Raigne

BY WRITT OF PRIVY SEALE
PIGOTT

APPENDIX II

The Bylaws of 1670

THE WORSHIPFUL Company of Wheelwrights came into being by virtue of the Royal Charter of 3 February 1670 but was in fact almost powerless to act until the bylaws had been approved. The regulations and actions taken in the first forty years of the Company's life were based on the 'Rules and Ordinances of the Wheelwrights' Company', officially signed and sealed on 12 October 1670. To assist the understanding of the Company's history these bylaws, and the reason for them, are reproduced in full.

TO ALL TO WHOME THIS PRESENT Writing shall come Sir ORLANDO BRIDGEMAN KNIGHT and BARONETT Lord Keeper of the great Seale of England Sir MATHEW HALES Knight Chiefe Justice of the Court of King's Bench and Sir JOHN VAUGHAN Knight Chiefe Justice of the Court of Common Pleas Send Greeting

WHEREAS in and by a certaine Act of Parliament made in the Nyneteenth yeare of the raigne of King Henry the Seaventh Itt is amongst other things Enacted that no Masters Wardens or Fellowships of Crafts or Misteries or any of them or any Rulers of Guilds or Fraternitres shall take upon them to make any acts or ordinances nor execute or use any act or ordinance by them heretofore made in disinherison or diminucion of the King's prerogative or any other or against the Common Weale or proffitt of the King's Subjects & liege people except the same acts or ordinances be examined and approved by the Chancellor and treasurer of England or the Chiefe Justices of either Bench or three of them or else before both the Justices of Assize in their Circuites or progresses in that Shire where such acts and ordinances be made Upon the paine of Forfeiting forty pounds for every time they doe thereunto Contrary as in the said act it doth more plainely appeare

THE Masters Wardens & Assistants of the Company of Wheelwrights of the City of London willing and desiring the said act in every behalfe to be observed and kept the twelveth day of October in the two and twentieth yeare of the raigne of our Soveraigne Lord King CHARLES the SECOND over England &c HAVE Exhibited and presented theire humble peticion unto Us with this present writeing Containeing the rules and ordinances by them ordained devised and made for the said Company and theire Successors and for the Common Weale Conservacion of the good estate of the mistery of the said Wheelewrights AND thereupon have Instantly desired Us that wee would peruse and Examine the said orders & rules & ordinances & approve the same

WHEREUPON in pursuance of the said Act of Parliament We have perused the said ordinances the Tenor whereof hereafter ensue and follow vizt

INPRIMIS Whereas it hath pleased his said most Excellent Majesty King CHARLES the SECOND that now is over England &c. of his especiall grace and favour by his highnes Letters patents beareing date att Westminster the third day of February in the two and twentieth yeare of his Majestyes raigne to make them a body Corporate and politique and to Consist of a Master two Wardens & eighteene Assistants & Commonalty by the name of the Master Wardens Assistants & Commonalty of the Art and Mistery of Wheelewrights of the City of London And the manner and Choyce of the said Masters Wardens & Assistants in the said letters patents are expressed and sett downe for the better order to be held amongst the said Company now Incorporated Itt is hereby ordained that the Master Wardens and Assistants now nominated and appointed by his said Majestyes lettres patents soe to bee and their successors which hereafter shall bee Chosen into the said severall & respective offices shall before they enter upon the Execucion of their said severall and respective offices Take the respective oathes hereafter appoynted by these ordinances for every of them to take respectively.

ITEM it is agreed that the second Thursday of Every month shall be the usuall and ordinary Court dayes for the Master Wardens and Assistants of this Company and upon Every of those dayes a Court to bee held att the Hall or other meeteing place of the said Company within the City of London and if occasion doe require then such Court or assembly to be oftener and att such times as by the Master and Wardens of the said Company shall bee thought fitt and cause the same to bee summoned and alsoe an assembly or generall Court or Courts the same generall Courts to be appoynted & Summoned when as often as need shall require by the appoyntment of the Master and Wardens of the said Society

And of these, foure shall bee quarter dayes the same to be held yearely, one of them upon the first Thursday of January if the same shall not happen upon New yeares day, which if soe, then upon the day Followinge, the second Court upon the first Thursday of Aprill Except such Thursday be the Thursday next before Easter day which if it bee then upon the thursday in the weeke Following, The third Court upon the first Thursday in July And the fourth upon the first Thursday in October all of the said Courts to be kept att the Common Hall or other meeting place of the said Company within the City of London.

ITEM that on every of the said quarter dayes or court dayes every person that shall with his owne consent be admitted a Freeman of the said Fellowship or Incorporacion shall then and there satisfy & pay for quarterage twelve pence in money every quarter to the Master of the said Company for the time being to the use of the said Fellowshipp and every jornyman that shall by his owne consent be admitted a Freeman of the said Company shall pay for quarterage the summe of six pence per quarter and shall perform all such other Lawfull & reasonable orders rights and dutyes to the said Fellowship as by every other Fellow of the said Company ought to be done and that every person useing the trade of a Wheelwright in the Citty of London & Five miles Compasse thereof shall become member of this Society according to His Majesties Letters patents in that behalfe required.

ITEM that for every person by his owne Consent admitted into the said Fellowship makeing default of payment aforesaid and every person that shall make default of appeareance after reasonable Summons & Warninge to him given to bee att the said Courts or meetings att any time not haveing a reasonable excuse or departing from the same without leave of the said Court or Master of the said Company without some just & reasaonable cause shall Forfeit the respective summes of money hereafter following that is to say the Master or any of the Wardens not appeareing there by the houre appoynted before the Court is ended two shillings and for not comeing att all five shillings and every one of the Assistants of the said Company soe offending shall forfeite for comeing too late one shilling and for not comeing att all two shillings and sixpence and every other member by his owne consent admitted into the said Company or Fellowship as aforesaid soe sommoned or warned and not appeareing there att the houre appoynted shall forfeit one shilling and not comeing att all to the said Court or departing thence without licence before the Court be ended two shillings and if the Master or any of the Wardens or Assistants shall appeare att any of the said Courts or meetings not being decently habited and attyred he shall forfeit five shillings for every such time and every such other person admitted as aforesaid into the said Society refuseing denying or neglecting to pay his quarterage att any of the said quarter dayes or Courts after a personall demand to him or them made to pay the same shall loose and forfeit tenn shillings for every such default except the same shall bee moderated and dispensed with by a Court of Assistants of the said Company.

ITEM Such persons respectively who shall be Master and Wardens of the said Company shall respectively dureing the time of their being in the respective places or offices of Master or Warden shall use imploy and dispose all and every such summe or summes of money Rents Plate and other things and goods belonging to the said Company which they shall respectively receive bee possessed of or any way come to their respective hands or custody dureing the time of their beeing respectively Master or Wardens as shall be directed ordered and appoynted by the Court of Assistants for the time being from time to time and not otherwise and that after the Expiracion of their respective times of mastershipp or wardenshipp they shall respectively make and deliver to the use of the said Company a perfect true and full Account to and before such persons and att and by such seasonable time or times as by a Court of Assistants shall bee for such purpose nominated and appointed and after such Account soe made what shall bee found remaineing in their respective hands or custody belonging to the Company they shall respectively without dimunicion Covin or delay deliver att such time and place and to such persons and persons to the use of the said Company as by a Court of Assistants shall bee appointed.

ITEM itt is further Ordered that if any person Freeman of this Company shall be agreed upon as aforesaid to bee chosen Master or Warden of the said Company shall upon notice thereof deny refuse or neglect to take the same upon him that then he shall forfeite the summe of tenn pounds and then after there shall bee a proceeding to a new choice and eleccion of another in his place in like sort as shall bee done when any Master or Warden shall decease in the Terme of his said Office or as if such had been never soe elected

And that like proceeding shall bee had upon or against every person who shall bee chosen one of the Assistants and shall refuse or neglect to take upon him to bee of the Assistants and give his attendance as other of the Assistants doe in which case the Assistant or Assistants soe elected and refusing to hold the said Office as aforesaid shall forfeite and pay to the use of the Company the summe of Five pounds.

ITEM itt is Ordered that all persons admitted members of this Society shall make their Wheeles and other Ware Exposed to sale good well and substantiall and of good and substantiall materialls upon such paines and penaltyes as the Company or Court of Assistants may lawfully inflict upon them not exceeding Forty shillings.

ITEM itt is hereby Ordained that noe person or persons whatsoever following or useing the Trade of a Wheelewright shall presume to sett up shopp to follow the said Trade of a Wheelewright within the Citty of London or libertyes thereof or five miles compasse of the same unlesse he or they have served as an Apprentice by the space of seaven years to the said calling or trade of a Wheelewright according to the statute in that behalfe made in the Fifth year of the reigne of Queen Elizabeth of famous memory upon paine of being proceeded against for their contempt in this behalfe according to law and justice

And that noe person member of this Society shall make any dray or Coach Wheeles in any Brewers or Coachmakers house shopp or yard but onely in his owne house open shopp or yard upon the penalty of Forty shillings for every day they or any of them shall doe the contrary.

ITEM Whereas there are certaine persons in and about the Citty of London and Libertyes thereof and parts adjacent that doe buy Wheeles of severall Wheeleswrightes members of this Society before the same are fully finished That is to say before the boxes are putt in and Shooes putt upon the same in doeing whereof for want of knowledge in the said Art or Mistery itt being a principall part of the same they many times utterly spoyle the said goods and make the said wheeles which possibly before might be good and sufficient and fitt for sale altogether unfitt for service

Whereby gentlemen and others are not onely very much deceived in the goodnes of the Commoditye itt selfe but doe alsoe pay much the dearer for their wheeles in buying them att the second hand Itt is hereby Ordained that noe person or persons whatsoever admitted Member of this Society doe presume to sell or make any wheeles to or for any person or persons whatsoever and deliver the same unlesse itt bee to and for some Wheelwright to bee further wrought and perfected untill they bee boxed and shodd and finished fitt for use under the penalty of Forty shillings for every paire of wheeles by him or them soe sold and not finished boxed and shodd as aforesaid to bee paid to the use of this Fellowshipp.

ITEM that if att any time hereafter notice and command shall bee given to this Company to furnish His Majestyes Trayne of Waggons or Artillery with wheelwrights to attend the service thereof Thereupon this Company shall appoint fitt and able persons admitted of this Society for the said worke Iff thereupon any such Member shall refuse neglect or omitt to doe his duty therein as hee shall bee thereunto appointed by the Master Wardens and Assistants of this Company hee shall forfeite and pay to the use of this Company the summe of Five pounds over and besides such other paines and penaltyes as by His Majestye shall bee lawfully inflicted upon every such Offender in this behalfe.

ITEM noe person admitted a member of this Society shall hire receive or take or entertaine to Apprentice any person formerly Apprentice to any person of this Society without the consent of his next former Master if any such bee before his time is expired or before hee bee lawfully discharged by or from his next former Master upon paine that every person offending contrary to the true meaning of this Article shall for such offence forfeite twenty shillings and after notice to him or them soe offending given shall forfeite and pay for every month hee or they shall continue such Apprentice contrary to the true meaning of this Article the summe of Forty shillings.

ITEM that all summes of money limitted to bee imposed by these Ordinances or by vertue or force of these Ordinances by way of dutyes Forfeitures fines and penaltyes or otherwise att any time or times hereafter for any transgressions or offences contrary to any of these Ordinances or any lawfull Ordinances hereafter to bee made by this Society and which shall bee confirmed and approved according to the lawes and Statutes of this Realme shall bee by the Master Wardens Assistants recovered by Accion of Debt or levyed by distresse of the Offendors Goods by Warrant of the Court of Assistants to bee holden for this Company And shall bee and continue for ever to the use of this Fellowshipp to bee Imployed for the support and maintenance of the said Fellowshipp and to the poore and other charitable uses of this Fellowshipp and to bee paid to the Master or one of the Wardens of this Fellowshipp from time to time for the time being.

ITEM Every person that shall be admitted a Freeman of this Society shall pay for his or their Admittance thereinto to the use of the said Company thirteene shillings foure pence, to the Clerke three shillings foure pence, and to the Beadle one shilling six pence.

ITEM to the end that itt shall appeare what Oath or oathes every person or persons which shall become Master and Wardens or of the Assistants or a Freeman of this Company or Fraternity or the Clerke or Beadle shall take or enter into It is Ordered and Ordained that they shall severally and respectively take the severall Oathes here ensueing That it is to say every of them to take the oathes of Supremacye and Allegiance to and of the King's Majestye his heires and Successors according to the lawes of this Realme as they now are or hereafter shall bee provided.

ITEM every Master and Warden agreed upon and chosen to bee

Master and Warden for the succeeding yeare shall take his Oathe before the Master and both or one of the Wardens for the preceding yeare and Court of Assistants to the effect ensueing vizt

You shall bee true to our Soveraigne Lord the King and to his heires and Successors You shall Endeavour your selfe the best you can whilest you continue in this Office whereunto you are now chosen justly and indifferently to execute and cause to be executed your Office in every respect and to put in due execucion all the good and lawfull Ordinances herein expressed and conteyned as farre forth as by law you may without assesseing or punishing any person for envy hatred or malice or spareing any person for reward dread favour or affecion And all and every plate goods jewells summes of money or any other thing or things that by reason of your said Office shall come to your hands charge or custody to the use of or belonging to the said Fellowshipp you shall according to the Ordinances and direccions made touching the same yeild and make a good true and plaine Accompt within convenient time after you shall bee thereunto required by the Master and Wardens of this Company for the time being Soe helpe you God.

ITEM for every one chosen from time to time to bee of the Assistants to bee taken before the Master and both or one of the Wardens and Court of Assistants to the effect ensueing vizt

You shall sweare to bee true to our Soveraigne Lord the King and to his heires and Successors You shall assist the Master and Wardens of this Company or Fellowshipp of Wheelewrights for the time being in their Oversight rule and Government of the said Company or Fellowshipp soe long as you shall continue one of the Assistants of the said Fellowshipp with your best and soundest advice and Councell and shall endeavour your selfe to the utmost of your skill and knowledge justly and indifferently to execute your said place and Office in every respect and to put in due execucion all the good and lawfull Ordinances of this Society in the Charter and booke of Ordinances expressed and conteined as farre forth as lawfully you may and shall not punish or assesse any person for hatred or malice or spare any person for love dread favour or affeccion or hope of reward Soe helpe you God.

ITEM the Clerke of this Company or Fellowshipp shall take the oath in manner aforesaid and the effect ensueing vizt

You shall bee true to our Soveraigne Lord the King and to his heires and Successors and to the Master Wardens and Fellowshipp of this Society and all the Commandements of the Master and Wardens being lawfull and honest touching the affaires and business of this Fellowshipp belonging to your Office to your power as farre forth as lawfully you may you shall doe and Execute true Entryes of all things belonging to your Office you shall make without any partiallity favour or affeccion lucre or gaine Envy hatred or malice whatsoever you shall not knowingly and willingly doe and committ anything that may be hurtfull or prejudiciall to the said Master Wardens and fellowshipp but shall honestly justly and truely execute your office of Clerkeshipp in all things apperteining to the same as the Clerke of the said Master Wardens and Fellowshipp of this Society ought to doe soe long as you shall continue and be in the same office according to your best skill power and ability without any partiallity Soe helpe you God.

ITEM every one which shall bee att a Court of Assistants chosen and allowed to be a Beadle of this Company or Fellowshipp and Society shall take his oath in manner aforesaid and to the effect ensueing vizt

You shall be true to our Soveraigne Lord the King's Majestye and to his heires and Successors and obedient shall bee to the Master and Wardens of this Fellowshipp for the time being their Commandements lawfull and honest touching the affaires and busines of this Company to the uttermost of your power willingly you shall doe as farre as lawfully you may and generally you shall justly and truely doe and execute all & everything and things apperteineing to the said office of Beadle as the Beadle of the said Master Wardens and Fellowshipp ought to doe to the uttermost of your knowledge skill power and ability soe long as you shall continue in the said office without partiality Soe helpe you God.

ITEM every one that shall hereafter bee received to bee a Freeman or member of this Company shall take his oath in the manner aforesaid and to the effect heere Ensueing vizt

You shall sweare to bee true to our Soveraigne Lord the King's Majesty and to his heires & Successors and att all times obedient to the Master and Wardens of this Fellowshipp and Society and their Successors after them in all honest and lawfull things touching the affaires and busines of this Fellowshipp If you shall knowe any manner of meeteing Conspiracyes plotts or devises against the King's Majesty his heires or Successors you shall to the uttermost of your power hinder the same and speedily disclose the same to the Master or one of the Wardens of this Society and this City of London & Fellowshipp of Wheelewrights you shall keepe harmless as much as in you lyeth and as by law you may Soe helpe you God.

AND LASTLY it is hereby ordained and appointed that these ordinances be openly read once in every yeare att a quarter Court of Assistants to bee holden before the Master Wardens and Assistants of this Society or the major part of them on the first Thursday in Aprill every yeare Successively to the end that no member of this Society may pretend Ignorance of the same WHICH said ordinances in manner and forme before specifyed att the request of the said Master Wardens & Assistants of the aforesaid Mistery of Wheelewrights by Authority of the aforemencioned Act of Parliament Wee the said Lord Keeper and Chiefe Justices of either Bench aforesaid have Examined

AND the same ordinances as farre as wee lawfully may in order to Exempt the said Company from the penalty of the said Statute in that Case made and provided Wee doe by these presents approve

In WITNESSE Whereof Wee have hereunto Subscribed our names and put our Seales.

L.S.	L.S.	L.S.
Orld Bridgemen	Mathew Hales	John Vaughan
Lord Keeper	C.J. of the	C.J. of the
	King's Bench	Common Pleas

K

These were the rules which governed the Company for the first forty-three years of its existence. A new set of ordinances, incorporating the regulations made by the Company in that period and making some additions to and variations of the original bylaws were drawn up in October 1713 and approved in April 1714. (Given in full in Appendix III.)

APPENDIX III

The Bylaws of 1714

ORDERS RULES ACTS and ORDINANCES

Ordinances made
22 Oct. 1713

sealed 1 April
1714

allowed 3 April
1714

declared devised and made by WILLIAM DAY Master and NATHANIEL GOODWIN and THOMAS WEST Wardens and the Assistants and Commonalty of the Art and Mistery of WHEEL-WRIGHTS of the City of London at a COURT holden by them at PLAISTERER'S HALL in Addle Street London the Twenty second day of October in the year of our Lord One Thousand and Seven hundred and Thirteen And in the Twelfth year of the Reign of our Soveraign Lady ANNE Queen of Brittain France and Ireland Defender of the Faith &c. for the well Government of the said COMPANY and TRADE

FIRST It is ORDAINED that the Master Wardens and Assistants of the said Company and their Successors for ever shall and may at all times hereafter at their Wills and Pleasure by the appointment of the Master and Wardens of the said Company for the time being upon due Summons Congregate and Assemble themselves together and keep Courts at their Common Hall or other convenient place of meeting within the City of London or Liberties thereof and they or the greatest part of them whereof the Master and one of the Wardens shall be two shall be and be called a COURT of ASSISTANTS as well for the better Ordering Ruling and Governing of the said Company and the Members thereof and all others that use practice and Exercise the said Trade of a Wheelwright within the Cities of London and Wesminster or within Five Miles any ways distant from the same as for Correction Redresse and Reformacion of abuses which may be committed touching the said Trade of a Wheelwright or any part thereof

AND also shall and may yearly and every year keep Four Quarterly Courts upon such days as are hereinafter mencioned (vizt) One of them upon the first Thursday in January if the same shall not happen upon New Year's Day But if the same shall so happen Then upon the Thursday following The second Quarterly Court day upon the first Thursday in April Except it be the Thursday before Easter which if it be Then on the

Thursday in the week following The Third Quarterly Court upon the first Thursday in July And the Fourth Quarterly Court upon the first Thursday after the Twenty ninth day of September Unto which Courts it shall and may be lawfull for the Master and Wardens to Summons by their Beadle or other Officer all the Members of the said Company To the intent they may then and there hear the Orders of the said Company that all who are concerned to obey the same may be left inexcusable And if any Member of the said Company refuse or neglect to appear at any such Court or Meeting (being duly Summoned and not having a reasonable Excuse) every such person shall forfeit and pay to the Master and Wardens Assistants and Commonalty of the said Company Three shillings and four pence of lawfull money of Great Brittain for every such default.

ITEM It is Ordained and declared That the Master Wardens and Assistants of the said Company of Wheelwrights for the time being and their Successors for ever shall and may on the first Thursday after the Nine and Twentieth day of September yearly Assemble and meet together And shall and may Elect and Choose one Master out of the Wardens or Assistants of the said Company who have served the office of Warden And two Wardens out of the Assistants of the said Company for the then next ensuing year and untill others shall be Elected and sworn into the same respective Places according to Direccions and Limittacions of the Charter to them granted bearing the date at Westminster the Third day of February in the Twenty second year of the Reign of King Charles the Second Which said persons so Elected and chosen shall upon due notice thereof appear at a Court to be held within Fourteen days then next And then and there shall take the Oath hereby appointed according to the direccions of the Charter of the said Company And also on that day at their own Costs and charges make and provide a competent and sufficient Dinner for the Master Wardens and Assistants of the said Company

And each and every person or persons so Elected Master or Warden that shall refuse or neglect to appear at such Court and take upon him such Office respectively not having a reasonable excuse for such his neglect or refusall or shall fail to make such Dinner or pay his proportion of the charges of the same shall forfeit and pay to the Master Wardens Assistants and Commonalty of the said Company the Sum of Ten pounds of lawfull money of Great Brittain.

ALSO It is Ordained and declared That the Master Wardens and Assistants of the said Company shall and may from time to time as occasion shall require Elect and choose able and sufficient persons of the Company not exceeding Eighteen at any one time to be Assistants to the said Master and Wardens of the said Company according to the direccions and Limitacions of the said Charter And every person and persons so Elected shall upon due notice to him given appear at the next Court of Assistants to be held for the said Company and then and there take the Oath in these presents appointed for that purpose before the Master Wardens and Assistants of the said Company or any Five of them

And upon his Admission to the said Place shall for the better support of the said Company pay to the Master of the said Company for the use of the said Company the sum of Ten pounds and to the Clerk for administring the Oath Two shillings and Sixpence and to the Beadle one shilling

And if any persons or persons so Elected and chosen an Assistant shall after due notice given him neglect or refuse to appear and to take upon him or them the same place as is aforesaid and make such payments as aforesaid not having a reasonable Excuse for such his neglect or refusall such person or persons so neglecting or refusing shall forfeit and pay to the Master Wardens Assistants and Commonalty of the said Company the full Sum of Twenty pounds of lawfull money of Great Brittain.

AND also It is Ordained that within Twenty days after the Election or Admission of a new Master and Wardens the last Master and Wardens and every of them respectively shall (upon due notice given them of the time and place appointed them for that purpose and not having a reasonable Excuse for not doing the same) give a true and perfect Account in writing unto such persons as shall be appointed Auditors for that purpose by the Court of Assistants or the major part of them assembled of for and concerning all moneys Plate Goods Writings and other things that shall have come to his or their hands or Custody belonging to the said Company

And shall upon Auditing such Account pay and deliver the same moneys Plate Goods Chattells Writings and other things remaining in his or their hands to the Master of the Company for the time being for the use of the said Company upon pain that every person and persons refusing or neglecting so to do not having a reasonable Excuse for such his refusall or neglect shall forfeit and pay to the Master Wardens Assistants and Commonalty of the said Company the Sum of Five pounds of lawfull money of Great Brittain for every week that he or they shall detain any of the premisses in his or their hands or Custody.

ALSO It is Ordained that every year yearly the Master Wardens and Assistants of the said Company for the time being shall and may Elect and Choose Three fit persons of the said Company (who have not served the Office of Steward or paid a fine for not serving the same) to be and to have and bear the Title and Office of Stewards of the said Company who shall for the honor of the said Company at their the said Stewards' own costs and charges make and provide Two competent and sufficient Dinners one of which shall be called the Steward's Dinner And shall be provided and kept on the day that the Lord Mayor shall be sworn at Westminster and shall be for the Master Wardens and Assistants and such of the said Company as shall be called to attend them upon that occasion And the other Dinner shall be yearly provided as aforesaid and kept on the day of Election of new Master and Wardens And shall be for the Master Wardens and Assistants of the said Company

And every person so Elected Steward and having due notice of the same That shall refuse to hold and Execute the same place or fail to make such Dinners or pay his proporcion of the charges of the same not having a reasonable Excuse for such his neglect or refusall shall forfeit and pay to the Master Wardens Assistants and Commonalty of the said Company the Sum of Twenty pounds of lawfull money of Great Brittain.

ALSO It is Ordained that no Bill Bond Lease or other Writing shall pass under the Common Seale of the said Company but by order of the Master Wardens and Assistants of the said Company for the time being or the major part of them and in a Court of Assistants And every person to whose Custody the same Seale shall be intrusted who shall permit the same to be used in any other manner shall for every offence Forfeit and pay to the Master Wardens Assistants and Commonalty of the said Company the Sum of One hundred pounds of lawfull mony of Great Brittain and the Damages which the said Company shall sustain by such setting to of the Seal and shall be disabled to hold any place or Office in the said Company after.

ALSO It is Ordained That the Master Wardens and Assistants of the said Company for the time being shall and may from time to time Elect and Choose such persons of the Yeomandry of the said Company as they shall think fit to attend the Master Wardens and Assistants of the said Company as Ushers at such times as the said Company shall be Summoned to attend the Lord Mayor of London for the Honour and Grandeur of the said City on the day that he is sworn at Westminster or upon any other solemn occasion And if any person being so Elected shall refuse or neglect to attend and perform the said Service not having a reasonable Excuse for such his refusall or neglect every such person so offending shall forfeit and pay to the Master Wardens Assistants and Commonalty of the said Company the Sum of Thirty shillings of lawfull money of Great Brittain.

ALSO It is Ordered and Ordained That all the Members of the said Company shall upon Summons by the Beadle or other Officer attend on every Quarter Court Day that shall be held by or for the said Company And shall then and there pay unto the Under Warden of the said Company for the time being or such other person as shall be appointed to receive the same by the Court of Assistants or the major part of them for and in the name of Quarteridge money the respective sums of mony following (that is to say) The Master Wardens Assistants and all other Members of the said Company shall pay every one the Sum of Twelve pence a Quarter (Except such who are or shall be Working Journeymen) and such Working Journeymen to pay Six pence a Quarter and no more so long as they shall be Working Journeymen only towards the support of the said Company.

ALSO It is Ordained and Ordered That from henceforth it shall not be lawfull for any person or persons of the said Company to have and keep more Apprentices at one time than is hereafter limitted (that is to say) the Master and Wardens and such who have been Master or Wardens may have and keep Two Apprentices at one time and no more And all other the Assistants of the said Company may have and keep two Apprentices at one time and no more. And all other persons Members of the said Company that is or shall have been five years made Free may have and keep one Apprentice at one time and no more And that every person that shall do contrary shall forfeit and pay to the Master Wardens Assistants and Commonalty of the said Company such reasonable Fine as the Master Wardens and Assistants of the said Company or the Major part of them shall think fit not exceeding the Sum of Five pounds.

ALSO It is Ordained and Ordered that no Member of the said Com-

pany shall take any Apprentice or Apprentices but such as shall be presented
to the Master and one of the Wardens of the said Company and bound by
the Clerk of the said Company to a Free Wheelwright of the said Company
And every Master taking and binding such Apprentice shall pay to the
Master or Wardens of the said Company for the use of the said Company
Two shillings and Six pence upon pain that every person that shall refuse
so to do or do bind any Apprentice in any other manner shall pay and forfeit to the Master Wardens Assistants and Commonalty of the said Company the Sum of Forty shillings of lawfull money of Great Brittain.

ALSO It is Ordained that it shall not be lawfull for any Member of the
said Company to assign over his said Apprentice or to accept the Assign-
ment of the Apprentice of any other without the leave and consent of the
Master and one of the Wardens of the said Company for the time being
upon pain that every person that shall do the contrary shall forfeit and pay
to the Master Wardens Assistants and Commonalty of the said Company
the sum of Five pounds of lawfull money of Great Brittain.

ALSO It is Ordained and Ordered that all and every person and persons
that shall hereafter be admitted into the Freedom of the said Company
shall pay to the Master or Wardens for the use of the said Company the
sum of Thirteen shillings and Four pence of lawfull money of Great Brittain
And to the Clerk Three shillings and Four pence And to the Beadle one
shilling and sixpence of like lawfull money.

ALSO It is Ordained and Ordered That no person or persons whatsoever Members of this Company do for the future presume to make any
Wheel or Wheels but of good and Sound Timber and Substantiall Materialls
upon pain of Forfeiting to the Master Wardens Assistants and Commonalty
of the said Company the Sum of Twenty shillings for every Offence.

ALSO It is Ordained that no person or persons whatsoever being Members of the said Company shall make any Dray Cart or Coach Wheeles in
any Brewers or Coachmakers or Woodmongers House Shop or Yard upon
pain of Forfeiting to the Master Wardens Assistants and Commonalty of the
said Company the Sum of Forty shillings a day for every day he shall do or
Act contrary.

ALSO It is Ordained that no person or persons whatsoever being Members of this Company shall presume to sell or make any Wheeles to or
for any person or persons whatsoever and deliver the same (unless it be for
some Wheelwright to be further wrought and perfected) untill they be
boxed and Shod and finished fit for use upon pain of forfeiting to the Master
Wardens Assistants and Commonalty of the said Company the Sum of
Forty shillings for every pair of Wheels that shall be sold or delivered and
not finished Boxed and Shod as aforesaid.

ALSO It is Ordained and Ordered that no person or persons being a
Member of the said Company shall intice procure receive or take into his
her or their service the Apprentice of any other Member of the said Company And if any Member shall retain and keep in his service the Apprentice of any other Member without the consent of his Master after notice to
him given Shall forfeit and pay to the Master Wardens Assistants and
Commonalty of the said Company the Sum of Forty shillings a Week for

every Week he or they shall so retain and keep such Servant or Apprentice after such notice as aforesaid.

ALSO It is Ordained that it shall and may be lawfull for the Master Wardens and Assistants of the said Company or the major part of them at all times hereafter at their Court of Assistants to Admit and take into their Company any person or persons to be made free of the said Company by way of Redempcion according to the Directions and Limittacions of the said Charter And that the Master and Wardens and Court of Assistants shall receive and take of every such person and persons which shall by them be admitted accepted or received such like Fees and Duties as of late time have been used to be paid and received upon such Admittance for the use of the said Company.

ALSO It is Ordained that no Member of the said Company shall malitiously disparage or undervalue another Member in his Work or Trade nor shall any such person revile any other member or use any sinister or unlawfull means to obtain another member's Customer upon pain that every person that shall do to the contrary shall forfeit and pay to the Master Wardens Assistants and Commonalty of the said Company the Sum of Forty shillings of lawfull money of Great Brittain.

ALSO It is Ordained and Ordered that the Master Wardens and Assistants for the time being or the major part of them in a Court of Assistants shall and may according to their discretions mitigate or wholly remit any Fine or penalty imposed or set upon any Members of the said Company for breach of any Ordinance or otherwise howsoever.

ALSO It is Ordained and Ordered that no person or persons whatsoever Members of the said Company do hereafter make any Wheel or Wheeles for any Carr or Cart Dishing beyond the Face of the Wheel Nave And that the Sweep of the said Wheeles exceed not Eight inches and Nine inches in depth and not above Six inches and an half in thicknesse And that no Axle Tree of any such Carr exceed three foot Ten inches under the Body of the Cart upon pain of forfeiting to the Master Wardens Assistants and Commonalty of the said Company the sum of Twenty shillings for every Offence.

ALSO It is Ordained that the Master Wardens and Assistants of the said Company or any three or more of them whereof the Master or one of the Wardens to be always one shall and may in the daytime enter into any Shop House Workhouse or room or place whatsoever of all and every person and persons Members of the said Company there to search and try the wares workmanship and materialls used or wrought by any Wheelwright whether the same be fit for use or not and shall endeavour to find out all deceipts used and practiced in the said Trade according to the direccions and limittacions of the said Charter And all such as shall be found offenders to be dealth withall according to Law

And if upon any such Search there shall found any Insufficient wares Materialls or other deceipts That the person so offending shall forfeit and pay to the Master Wardens and Assistants and Commonalty of the said Company such Fines as shall be reasonably sett upon him or them by a Court of Assistants of the said Company the same not exceeding Twenty shillings of lawfull mony of Great Brittain And if any person or persons members of the said Company shall resist or be contumacious to the said Searchers or shall not permit or suffer them to make such Search as aforesaid That then every such person so offending shall forfeit and pay to the Master Wardens Assistants and Commonalty of the said Company the Sum of Five pounds of lawfull money of Great Brittain

AND for the more regular recovery of the severall penalties Forfeitures and Sums of money by the severall orders aforesaid imposed sett appointed or limitted to be paid

IT IS further ORDERED That the Master Wardens Assistants and Commonalty of the said Company for the time being shall and may Sue for the same in any of her Majesties Courts held within the City of London by Accion of Debt in the name of the Master Wardens Assistants and Commonalty of the Art and Mistery of Wheelwrights of the City of London according to the direccions and limittacions of the said Charter And the same when recovered shall be to the use of the said Company.

AND forasmuch as by the said Charter Oaths of Office are enjoyned to be Administred to the Master Wardens Assistants and Freemen of the said Company and to the Clerk and Beadle for the time being But no form of the said Oaths is therein specifyed IT IS further ORDERED that the severall hereafter following shall be accordingly Administred by the Master and Wardens and Assistants of the said Company or such of them as by the said Charter are Authorized and Impowered to Administer the same in the form and words herein set down and expressed

---

THE OATH to be taken by the Master
of the Company of Wheelwrights London

YOU shall Swear that you will be good and true to our Soveraign Lady Queen ANNE and to her Heires and lawfull Successors That you will be faithfull and True to the Company of Wheelwrights And that you as Master of the said Company will keep maintain and Execute and cause to be kept maintained and Executed and observed all the lawfull Ordinances and Orders of the said Company And of all Goods Plate Writings Sum and Sums of mony and all and every other thing and things whatsoever in any wise belonging to the said Company which shall come into your hands or possession you shall render a good true and faithfull Account to the best of your skill and knowledge

SO HELP YOU GOD

THE OATH to be taken by the
Wardens of the said Company

YOU and every of you shall swear that you will be good and true to our Soveraign Lady Queen ANNE and to her Heirs and lawfull Successors That you will be faithfull and true to the Company of Wheelwrights And that you will as Wardens of the said Company to the best of your skill so far as you lawfully may observe and keep all the good lawfull and laudable Acts and Ordinances of the said Company now made or hereafter to be made You shall to your best Endeavours receive or cause to be received to the use of the said Company all Fines and Amerciaments imposed on any Offenders by the Orders and By-Laws of this Company And of all Goods Plate Writings Sum and Sums of money and every other thing and things whatsoever in any wise belonging to the said Company which come to your hands and possession you shall render a good and true faithfull Account SO HELP YOU GOD

THE OATH to be taken by every
Assistant of the said Company

YOU shall Swear that you will be good and true to our Soveraign Lady Queen ANNE and to her Heirs and lawfull Successors That you will be faithfull and true to the Company of Wheelwrights You shall in all things relating to the said Company deal justly and indifferently without partiality And all the lawfull Councill and Secrets of this Company and the Trade Art or Mistery thereof you shall faithfully and truly keep You shall readily attend the Master and Wardens upon Summons by their Beadle or other Officers unlesse you shall be reasonably hindred SO HELP YOU GOD

THE OATH to be taken by every person
to be made Free of the said Company

YOU shall Swear that you will be good and true to our Soveraign Lady Queen ANNE and to her Heirs and lawfull Successors and in all matters and things lawfull and reasonable relating to the said Company You shall be obedient to the Master Wardens Assistants and Governors of this Company for the time being and their Successors and shall readily appear upon all Summons by their Beadle or other Officer (Except you have sufficient cause to be absent) All the Lawfull Acts Ordinances and Orders made or to be made for the Weale Rule and good Government of the said Company you shall to your Power observe and keep or else forthwith pay such Fines and Penaltys as you shall according to the said Ordinances forfeit by reason of your disobedience and breaking the same You shall not do any wrong to any Member of this Company in relation to the said Trade but shall behave your self in your said Trade well and honestly SO HELP YOU GOD

THE OATH to be taken by the
Clerk of the said Company

YOU shall Swear that you will be good and true to our Soveraign Lady Queen ANNE and to her Heirs and lawfull Successors and in all matters and things lawfull and reasonable relating to the said Company YOU shall be Obedient to the Master and Wardens of this Company for the time being and their Successors And the Commandments of the Master and Wardens being lawfull and honest you shall do and Execute True Entrys of all things belonging to your Office you shall make without any partiality favour or affection for Lucre or Gaine Envy Hatred or Malice You shall not knowingly and willingly do or Comitt anything that may be hurtfull or prejudiciall to the said Master and Wardens and Company but shall truly Execute your Office of Clerk in all things appertaining to the same as you ought to do so long as you shall continue in the said Office according to your best Skill power and Knowledge SO HELP YOU GOD

———————

THE OATH to be taken by the
Beadle of the said Company

YOU   shall Swear that you will be good and true to our Soveraign Lady Queen ANNE and to her Heirs and lawfull Successors You shall be obedient to the Master Wardens and Assistants of the said Company for the time being and their Successors in all matters and things lawfull concerning your Place and Office of Beadle You shall lawfully warn to all Courts and Meetings all and every person and persons as you shall be by them appointed and give and return true Account of their Answers if you shall be thereunto required without spareing any for fear favour or affection reward or hope of gaine And as much as in you lyeth you shall behave your self well and orderly so long as you shall continue in your Office of Beadle SO HELP YOU GOD

Sealed with the Common Seal of the Company 1st April 1714	FOR the more Solemn Declaracion and Ratificacion of all which Orders Rules Acts and Ordinances WEE the said Master Wardens Assistants and Commonalty of the Art and Mistery of the Wheelwrights of the City of London have hereunto affixed our Common Seal in a Court of Assistants held at Plaisterers Hall in Addle Street London the First day of Aprill Thirteenth year of our said Soveraign Lady Queen ANNE ANNOQUE DOMINI 1714
Approved by the Lord Chancellor and the Chief Justices under the Statute of 19 Henry VII c.7 3rd April 1714	We have seen and perused these By-Laws and do approve allow & confirm the same Given under our Hands & Seals this Third day of April 1714

L.S.	L.S.	L.S.	L.S.
Company's Seal	Simon Lord Harcourt L.C.	Sir Thomas Parker Kt Court of Queen's Bench	Lord Trevor C.J. of the Court of Common Pleas

APPENDIX IV

The Company's Plate

A MINUTE of 22 February 1682 records: 'This day Matthew Bateman Esq., a Member of this Compaine, as a token of his love and kindness to the Compaine, did present them wth a large silver tankard, wch is to remaine wth the Compaine's Stock'.

Thus the first Master of the Company of Wheelwrights founded the Company's collection of plate—and founded a tradition of generosity to his brethren and to posterity.

1. THE BATEMAN TANKARD. A plain cylindrical silver tankard with cover, engraved with the Arms of the donor and inscribed 'Ye gift of Mr. Matthew Bateman to ye Company of Wheelwrights 1683'. Hallmarked 1682–3.

2. TWO SILVER RAT TAIL SPOONS, inscribed 'The gift of Mathias Bullen, 1683'. Hallmarked 1673. (Minute 22 November 1683: 'Mathias Bullen was this day admitted and sworne a member of this Corporation & pd his admittance fee, and gave the Compaine two large silver spoones in toaken of his good will to the Compaine.'

3. A SILVER CUP AND COVER, fluted base and stem, engraved border of scrolls at top and festoons in the centre, fluted cover with pineapple button, inscribed: 'This cup was presented to the Worshipful Company of Wheelwrights by Alexander Brander, Esqe., November 9th, 1792, Sheriff of the City of London and County of Middlesex, and late Master of this Company.' Hallmarked 1785.

4. A SILVER CUP AND COVER, elaborately chased with leaf and wreaths, engraved with the arms of the donor and inscribed: 'Presented by George Bridges, Esqr., Alderman of London and a Member of the Worshipful Company of Wheelwrights; elected Alderman in the year 1811, Sheriff in 1816, Mayor in 1819, and Representative of the City in Parliament 1820.' Hallmarked Birmingham 1818–9.

5. A SILVER GILT SNUFF BOX, engraved with the Company's Arms, inscribed 'The Gift of the late Mr. John Edwards'. He was Clerk to the Company from 1770 to 1791. Presented in 1791. Hallmarked 1781.

6. A SILVER GILT SNUFF BOX, engine-turned with flower border, inscribed (inside): 'Presented on the 30 Septr. 1841, to the Court of Assistants of the Worshipful Company of Wheelwrights, by Mr. B. W. Scott, their late Clerk, in testimony of the great respect entertained by him for several Members of the Court of the said Company.'

7. A SILVER CUP, gilt inside, engraved with the Arms of the Company, presented by Samuel Edward Donne in 1866, Master in 1868.

8. A SILVER CUP AND COVER, gilt inside, engraved with the Arms of the Company, presented by James Fortescue Harrison, Master in 1882.

9. TWO GILT AND CHASED ROSE-WATER DISHES, presented by John Runtz, Master in 1884.

10. A SILVER GILT TANKARD, chased with mask lip, presented by Walter Webb, Master in 1891.

11. A SILVER CIGAR WAGON, presented by Sir John Henry Puleston, MP, Master in 1886.

12. A SILVER CUP AND COVER, fluted with two handles, presented by John Johnson Runtz, JP, Master in 1898.

13. A SILVER GILT SALVER, with vine-leaf border, the centre chased with flowers and birds, presented by Francis Bowry Buckland, JP, Master in 1903.

14. A SILVER CUP AND COVER, presented by Colonel Thomas Horrocks Openshaw, CB, CMG, FRCS, Master from 1915 to 1918.

15. A SILVER CUP AND COVER, presented by Henry Oberlin Serpell, DL, JP, Master in 1920.

16. A SILVER MEMORIAL BOX, presented in 1919 by Thomas Harvey Hull, Clerk to the Company from 1908 to 1949, Master in 1937.

17. A SILVER SALVER, presented by Sir Randle Fynes Wilson Holme, Master in 1926.

18. A SILVER SALVER, left to the Company in 1948 under the will of Richard William Bowry Buckland, Master in 1930.

19. TWIN SILVER CUPS WITH COVERS, engraved with the Arms of the Company, presented by Andrew Money Woodman, CC, Master in 1954.

20. A SILVER CASKET, presented by Frederick William Charles Barker, MIStructE, LRIBA, Master in 1958.

21. A MASTER'S BADGE OF OFFICE, gold, enamelled in colours with the arms, crest and supporters of the Wheelwrights' Company, surrounded by a border of wheels and surmounted by the arms of the Corporation of the City of London, 1873.

22. A BEADLE'S STAFF, surmounted in silver with the Arms of the Company. 1774.

23. A POOR'S BOX, made of oak, The Company's Arms are represented on one side in iron, painted in heraldic colours. The date 1682 is placed one figure on each of the four sides, also in iron. (Minute of 22 February 1682: 'Mr. Warden Preston presented the Compaine wth a very handsome wainscott Box wch is to receive such money as shall be given for the releife of the poore.')

24. GOLD REPRODUCTION ELIZABETHAN GOBLET with applied Company's Coat of Arms in pierced gold and enamel for the use of the Master, presented by Col R. L. Broad, MC, Master in 1965.

25. GOLD AND ENAMEL CLERK'S BADGE, depicting Company's Coat of Arms, presented by Col E. G. Bates, MBE, TD, MA, LLB, Master in 1966

26. TWO SILVER REPRODUCTION ELIZABETHAN GOBLETS with applied Company's Coat of Arms in pierced silver and enamel for the use of the Wardens, presented by M. J. W. Russell, TD, Master in 1967.

27. Two Gold Reproduction Elizabethan Goblets with applied Company's Coat of Arms in pierced gold and enamel for the use of the Master, presented by Col R. L. Broad, MC, Master in 1965, to commemorate the Company's Tercentenary.

28. Silver Salver, engraved with the Company's Coat of Arms, presented by Liveryman E. Bruce Miller, to commemorate the Company's Tercentenary.

APPENDIX V

The Masters of the Worshipful Company of Wheelwrights

THE FIRST Master of the Company was appointed by the Royal Charter and held office until October 1670. Since the years of office overlap, the dates given are not those of installation but of the substantive year of office.

1670	Mathew Bateman	1698	James Kerby
1671	Ralph Ashby (died in office)	1699	Richard Smith
		1700	William Shallock
	Christopher Hawes	1701	Richard Clarke
1672	Christopher Hawes	1702	Edward Chapman
1673	Samuel Gynes	1703	Henry Graves
1674	Bartholomew Hooper	1704	John Bateman
1675	Richard Smart	1705	Thomas Granger
1676	James Mynn	1706	William Tame
1677	John Box	1707	Edmund Shelton
1678	William Duke	1708	Richard Sketchley
1679	James Timberlake	1709	John Farrington
1680	John Eades	1710	James Mynn (resigned)
1681	Henry Graves		James Kerby
1682	Hugh Emery	1711	Wm Tame
1683	Thomas Jackson	1712	James Ireland
1684	Edward Bussey	1713	Arthur Beard
1685	John Preston	1714	William Day
1686	John King	1715	Nathaniel Goodwin
1687	Thomas Long	1716	Thomas West
1688	Charles Hewitt	1717	John Hilliard
1689	James Mynn	1718	William Jones
1690	Edward Wade	1719	Cæsar Grainger
1691	William Harman	1720	John Sample
1692	Thomas Humfryes	1721	William Shelton
1693	Symon Collison	1722	Joseph Wright
1694	William Buck	1723	Thomas Jones
1695	Richard Greene	1724	William Gray
1696	John Harris	1725	Joseph Answorth
1697	William Symmons (died in office)	1726	Thomas Wheeler
		1727	John Bishop
	Mathew Bateman	1728	Jeremiah Davis

1729	John Haslam	1773	Richard Turrell (died in office)
1730	Edward Wilder		John Miles
1731	Edward Humphreys	1774	Samuel Hinds Harman
1732	John Horton	1775	James Hawkins
1733	John Linn	1776	Robert Webb
1734	Charles Pattison	1777	Edward Lloyd
1735	Thomas Wiseham	1778	William Caslake, Junr
1736	Joseph Clark	1779	John Newbold
1737	Thomas Brown	1780	Barnett Price
1738	Thomas Fullker	1781	Benjamin Worthy
1739	Richard Sharp	1782	John Font
1740	James Burges	1783	Robert Perryman
1741	Richard Baker	1784	James Rowley
1742	Benjamin Coster	1785	Robert Sparrow
1743	John Harris (died in office)	1786	Edward Parish
	John Bishop	1787	John Gardiner
1744	Edward Rabbats	1788	Richard Friend
1745	William Sadgrove	1789	William Windsor
1746	William Wright	1790	Robert Atkinson
1747	Edward West	1791	David Davidson
1748	John Miles	1792	Alexr. Brander
1749	John Howard	1793	Thos. Perryman
1750	William Taverner	1794	John Biggerstaff
1751	William Mayor	1795	Thomas Stevens
1752	John Arnold	1796	Josiah Champion
1753	John George Elliott (removed from office)	1797	Thos. P. Perryman
		1798	Thos. Gill
	John Sample	1799	Thos. Gill
1754	Edward Leech	1800	Robert Peckham
1755	William Ashford	1801	William White
1756	William Caslake	1802	James Wilson
1757	Thomas Bayley	1803	William Browning
1758	Henry Templer	1804	William Ellis
1759	Lea Butler	1805	Robert Lever
1760	Thomas Nottingham	1806	Christopher Thomas
1761	William King	1807	Thomas King
1762	John Font	1808	John Prested
1763	James Miller	1809	Thomas Parker
1764	John Kirk	1810	John Smith
1765	George Sweeting	1811	Charles Martin
1766	William Turner	1812	Michael Peter Touray
1767	John Burch	1813	John Treacher
1768	Samuel Leaver	1814	William McAndrew
1769	William Gardiner	1815	William Cordell
1770	Richard Wilson	1816	William Cass
1771	John Rabbats	1817	John Pearson
1772	Barrington Wood	1818	Edmund Fleming

Year	Name	Year	Name
1819	William Hopes	1866	Geo. Webb
1820	Joseph Hurcombe	1867	John Banyard Chaffey
1821	William Ruston	1868	Samuel Edward Donne
1822	John Pickering Peacock	1869	Benjamin Spilsbury
1823	Alexander Adam	1870	Daniel Krlew
1824	Joshua Hutchinson	1871	Richd. Augustus Whithall
1825	Daniel Weston	1872	John King Farlow
1826	Thos. Williams	1873	John Henry Machu
1827	Wm. Beer	1874	James Ebenezer Saunders, JP
1828	Sir Jas. Williams	1875	William Foster Newton (died in office) James Renat Scott
1829	Stephen Cleasby		
1830	John Soper		
1831	Jas. Browning		
1832	Josh. Munday	1876	William Clark
1833	Robert Day	1877	Robert Hy. Chas. Pallett
1834	Thos. Willis Cooper	1878	John Edensor
1835	Wm. Chaffers	1879	John Henry Dodson
1836	Wm. Beetham	1880	Ellis Jones
1837	Joseph Fleming	1881	Sir Edward William Watkin, Bart, MP
1838	Edward Conder		
1839	David Cameron	1882	Jas. Fortescue Harrison
1840	Edward Jones	1883	John Hughes
1841	George Wright	1884	John Rüntz
1842	Thos. Reece	1885	Charles Dew Miller
1843	William Northcote	1886	John Henry Puleston, MP
1844	Thos. Pallister	1887	Wm. George Lemon, JP
1845	James Templer	1888	Alfred Frank Aldridge
1846	Charles Rice	1889	Thomas Proctor Baptie, DL, JP
1847	John Watson		
1848	Joseph Starling	1890	Wm. John Rafferty
1849	John Chaffey	1891	Walter Webb
1850	Joseph Blades	1892	John Robbins
1851	E. Pallister	1893	Jas. Ebenezer Saunders, JP
1852	Richard Wilson	1894	Wm. Shepherd
1853	William Chaffers, Junr	1895	Hon Alan de Tatton Egerton, MP
1854	Thos. Joyce		
1855	Henry Baldwin	1896	John Coles, JP
1856	John Outhwaite	1897	Charles Cleverly Paine
1857	Jas. Browning	1898	John Johnson Runtz, JP
1858	William Chaffers	1899	William Mann Cross
1859	Ed. Conder, Sheriff of London and Middlesex	1900	Francis M. Mercer, FCS
		1901	Herbert E. Coles
1860	Henry Cameron	1902	Ezra T. Wilks, CC, FRGS
1861	Ed. Conder, Junr	1903	Francis B. Buckland, JP
1862	Henry Webb	1904	Henry T. Gordon, FRIBA, CC
1863	Wm. Robert Chalmers		
1864	Benjamin Scott	1905	Ald Sir George J. Woodman, JP, CC
1865	Wm. Brass		

L

1906	Henry J. Carter, JP	1942	Harold M. Moore, MC, FCA
1907	George E. Cockram		
1908	Sir George Peters, JP	1943	John d. Broad, FCA
1909	Josiah Gunton, FRIBA, CC	1944	Leonard R. Norris, LLB
		1945	Henry C. Bound, FCA
1910	Sir Percy Shepherd, CC	1946	Leslie E. Lawrie
1911	Henry D. Buckland	1947	James A. Chappell, CC
1912	Herbert H. Fuller	1948	Clifford Wilton
1913	George R. Higgins, JP	1949	A. Leslie Gordon, FRICS
1914	Albert E. Sabey	1950	Ernest A. Udall
1915		1951	Frank O. Wills, JP
1916	Colonel T. H. Openshaw,	1952	Lt-Colonel Herbert
1917	CB, CMG, FRCS		Brookhouse, MVO, CC
1918		1953	Major Guy Richardson, CC
1919	Martin L. Saunders		
1920	Henry O. Serpell, DL, JP	1954	Andrew M. Woodman, CC
1921	Frank E. Lemon, MA, LLB, JP	1955	C. D. King Farlow, MA, CC
1922	Rupert L. Norris, JP		
1923	Frank W. Robson	1956	H. Leonard Hunter
1924	Rt Hon Sir Kingsley Wood, MP	1957	Colonel Herbert J. Chappell, OBE, MC, TD
1925	John Lawrie		
1926	Sir Randle F. W. Holme	1958	Frederick W. C. Barker, MIStructE, LRIBA
1927	Sir Oliver Sheat, OBE, JP, CC	1959	Edwin A. Wormleighton
1928	Sydney C. Gordon	1960	Alfred S. Henderson, CC
1929	Charles A. Mercer	1961	Theodore A. Frankford
1930	Richard W. B. Buckland	1962	Frank L. Whitehead, FIOB
1931	Frankl. S. Wilks, OBE, FCA	1963	Arthur W. White, FCA
1932	Ald The Rt Hon Lord Ebbisham of Cobham, GBE	1964	Alderman H. Murray Fox, MA, FRICS, FAI
		1965	Lt-Col Richard Lowther Broad, MC
1933	Thomas B. Townson	1966	Lt-Col Eric George Bates, MBE, TD, MA, LLB
1934	Herbert A. Chappell, JP		
1935	Frank Durrant, FAI		
1936	Charles W. Rooke, FCA	1967	Michael John William Russell, TD
1937	T. Harvey Hull		
1938	John L. Baynes, CBE	1968	F. Griffiths Woollard, DL, JP
1939	Sir Sidney Fox, FRICS, FAI, CC		
		1969	Richard Edwin Stubington, FCA
1940	Victor Wilkins, FRIBA		
1941	Colonel Herbert C. Woodcock, TD, DL, JP	1970	Dr Geoffrey Sturt Udall, MA, MB, BChir, DCH

APPENDIX VI

Clerks to the Worshipful Company of Wheelwrights

1670	Thomas Johnson (dismissed December 1672)
1677	Thomas Johnson
1682	Robert Hyde
1709	Thomas Jackson
1730	Thomas Green
1757	James Green
1766	Joseph Bushnan
1767	Edward Bennett
1770	John Edwards
1791	Charles Montague
1818	Benjamin Whinnell Scott
1841	Benjamin Scott
1846	James Renat Scott
1870	James Benjamin Scott
1908	Thomas Harvey Hull
1949	H. W. Keith Calder, CBE, CC
1965	Michael H. Hinton, FCA

APPENDIX VII

Some Early Bonds

THESE ARE copies of some of the bonds given by Freemen and apprentices when setting up trade as a Wheelwright within the City or Liberties.

'*Noverint universi per presentes me Ricum Davis de Civit Westm Wheelewright teneri et firmiter Obliagari Witto Tame Civi et Wheelewright Londini in decem libris bonae et leglis monet Angliae   Solvend eidem Witto Tame aut suo certo Attornat Executorib suis, ad quam quidem soluconem bene et fidelit faciend Obligo me Executores at Administratores meos firmit per presentes Sigillo meo Sigillat dat 29° die Marcii Anno Regni dnae Annae nunc Reginae Angl etc quarto Annoque Dni 1705.*

'The Condicion of the Obligation above written is such that if the above Richd Davis shall at any time hereafter Sett up a Shopp and therein use & Exercise the trade or Occupation of a Wheelewright wth out the license and consent of the Master, Wardens and Assistants of the Compaine of Wheelewrights London that then he the said Richd Davis his Executors or Administrators shall and will pay or cause to be paid to him the said Wm. Tame to the use of the said Compaine the Summe of five pounds of Lawfull money of England, If therefore the said Richd Davis doth pay the summe of five pounds for the use of the said Compaine of Wheelewrights wthin one Month after he shall Sett up a Shopp wherein to use and Execute the Trade of Wheelewright, as aforesd then this Obligation to be voyd or els remaine in force.

The Marke of

Richd Davis

Sealed and delivered in
the presence of
      Robt Hyde
      James Timberlake.'

Here is another, this time all in good plain English:

'Know all Men by these Presents that *I Thomas Fidgeon of the parish of St. Olave's Southwark Wheelwright* am held and firmly bound to *James Burges Citizen and Wheelwright of London in Tenn pounds* of good and lawful Money of Great Britain to be paid to the said *James Burges* or his certain Attorney Executors Administrators or Assigns   For which Payment to be well and faithfully made *I* bind *myself my* Heirs Executors and Administrators firmly by these presents Sealed with my Seal. Dated the *Third* day of *July* in the *Fourteenth* year of the Reign of our Sovereign Lord *George the Second* by the Grace of God of Great Britain France and Ireland King Defender of the

Faith And in the year of our Lord One Thousand Seven Hundred and *Forty*.

'The Condition of this Obligation is such That if the above bound Thomas Fidgeon shall hereafter Sett up the Trade of a Wheelwright within the City of London or Five Miles distant from the same, Then if the said Thomas Fidgeon his Executors or Administrators do and shall well and truly pay or cause to be paid to one of the Wardens of the Company of Wheelwrights London for the time being to and for the use of the said Company the sum Five pounds of lawfull money of Great Britain within three months next after Setting up of the said Trade Then this Obligation shall be voyd Or else remain in full force and virtue.

Thomas Fidgeon.

Sealed and delivered (being first
duly stampt) in the presence of us
the words (Third and July) being first
inserted in the Obligation.

  Rih^d Hunterridge

  Thos Green.'

The third is evidently an undertaking by a new Freeman of the Company:

'Memorand I John Hayes doe hereby promise and Engage that if I shall and doe follow the Trade of a Wheelwright in the Cittie of London or five miles compass thereof after Midsomer next that then I will pay to the Master of the Companie of Wheelewrights the sume of five pounds of Lawfull English money. Witness my hand this 12th. day of February 1707.
Witness: John Hayes.

  Robt Hyde.'

Of those identifiable in these bonds, William Tame was Master of the Company in 1706 and again in 1711, James Timberlake was Master in 1679, and James Burges was Master in 1740.

Index